A Tough Act to Follow?

A Tough Act to Follow?

The Telecommunications Act of 1996 and the Separation of Powers

Harold W. Furchtgott-Roth

The AEI Press

Publisher for the American Enterprise Institute

WASHINGTON, D.C.

Distributed to the Trade by National Book Network, 15200 NBN Way, Blue Ridge Summit, PA 17214. To order call toll free 1-800-462-6420 or 1-717-794-3800. For all other inquiries please contact the AEI Press, 1150 Seventeenth Street, NW, Washington, DC 20036 or call 1-800-862-5801.

Library of Congress Cataloging-in-Publication Data
Furchtgott-Roth, Harold W.
    A tough act to follow : the Telecommunications Act of 1996 and the separa-
tion of powers / Harold Furchtgott-Roth.
        p. cm.
    Includes bibliographical references.
    ISBN 0-8447-4235-X (alk. paper)
1. Telecommunication policy—United States. 2. United States. Telecommunications Act of 1996. 3. United States. Federal Communications Commission.
4. Separation of powers—United States. 5. Telecommunication—Law and
legislation—United States. I. Title.

    HE7781.F87 2006
    384.0973—dc22

                                                            2005030557

10 09 08 07 06   1 2 3 4 5

Printed in the United States of America

To Diana

Contents

Acknowledgments

Many people have made this book possible, particularly my colleagues and friends at the American Enterprise Institute. I wrote the manuscript while I was a visiting fellow at AEI from June 2001 through March 2003. They have patiently waited for this book, and supported my efforts. Chris DeMuth, the president of AEI, has been more patient and provided better guidance than I had any reason to expect.

Some colleagues have suggested that I should update the book to reflect the many decisions and court defeats at the Federal Communications Commission since I completed research in late 2002. I can only plead laziness for not having done so. One of the tests of the value of an idea, however, is whether it holds over time. My conclusion, that separation of powers is a critical issue at the FCC, is no less true today than it was in late 2002. More recent evidence would corroborate, but not change, that conclusion.

Heather Dresser of AEI assisted me with the book in many different ways ranging from careful research assistance to coordinating the efforts of others who helped with parts of it, including Eliot Joel Rushovich of Harvard University. In addition, Simone Berkowitz of the Brookings Institute provided valuable research assistance.

I have learned much from my years of federal government service, both as a staff member and as an appointed official. To my colleagues at the Commission, I owe a debt of thanks. Bill Kennard, Susan Ness, Michael Powell, and Gloria Tristani both taught and tolerated me. The FCC staff taught me even more. Government employees are a hardworking, dedicated group. The problems of government, such as they are, are not the fault of staff. The FCC attracts many of the finest public servants. Neither the honesty nor the work ethic of the FCC commissioners and staff is at issue. Any group of people placed at the FCC will suffer from the structure of the agency; government simply cannot perform well without separation of powers, regardless of who is in it. These individuals are placed in an untenable position; they and the FCC can perform much better with a different agency structure.

I have also learned from members and staff of the House Commerce Committee, including Chairman Tom Bliley, James "J. D." Derderian, Michael Regan, Catherine Nolan, Justin Lilley, Ed Hearst, David Cavicke, and others. I owe a particular debt to my staff at the FCC. Paul Misener, Helgi Walker, Bryan Tramont, Rebecca Beynon, William Bailey, Robert Cailiff, Katie King, Ben Golant, and others taught me communications policy and communications law. Kevin Martin not only taught me well but he later became chairman of the Federal Communications Commission. Any good ideas in this book can likely be traced to these and other individuals who have advised me over the years. I have doubtlessly inserted errors where I have not fully learned from what they taught.

Those who know me well know that my memory is weak. Many individuals helped refresh my memory on various matters, reviewed parts of the book, and gave valuable advice. The reviewers include several colleagues at AEI: J. Gregory Sidak, Karlyn Bowman, Robert Hahn, and Chris DeMuth. Helpful comments also come from Robert Crandall, Thomas Hazlett, Bruce Owen, Bryan Tramont, William Trumbour, Jerry Udwin, and John Wohlstetter. To them I owe an enormous debt of gratitude. They made many suggestions to improve the manuscript. They also found many mistakes in the book that I have attempted to correct; the remaining mistakes are of my own creation.

Samuel Thernstrom managed both the publication of the book and the editing of the manuscript, which was done by Drew Helene and Lisa Ferraro Parmelee. Jenny Rowley of the Hudson Institute diligently found many of the footnotes.

Introduction

Congress rarely passes major new laws overhauling an agency. One recent example, however, was the Telecommunications Act of 1996 (the Act). That law substantially added to the responsibilities of the Federal Communications Commission (FCC), an independent agency that combines all of the powers of government.

The communications sector has been on an economic roller coaster since the passage of the Act. Hard times followed good times. The Act has been lionized in the good times and vilified in the bad. Yet it has never actually been followed. It is perhaps the fate of many laws not to be implemented precisely as Congress intended, but this piece of legislation is unusually distant—almost alien—from the actions taken in its name.

Many observers blame the Act in part for the poor performance of the communications sector, which is exposed daily to the regulations of the FCC under it. When economic conditions weaken, the government is a convenient and often irresistible target of blame.

Congress is not happy with the economic outcomes under the Act. Indeed, many of those who voted for it in 1996 are surprised by the evolution of the communications sector. Whether liberal or conservative, expectations of the implementation of the Act have not been fulfilled. Hardly anyone is pleased with it, despite ballooning FCC budgets. Perhaps the Act was too tough to follow.

As it considers rewriting the Act, Congress is getting plenty of advice about how to improve communications law. Practically all of it focuses on small refinements to policy: a little twist here, a little tightening there. Next time, perhaps, the FCC will implement the law better. What is needed now, or so most would-be advisors suggest, is an updated policy to reflect changes in technology.

This book suggests a different interpretation: Congress and the other branches of government will not be entirely satisfied with the FCC's implementation of any law as long as the agency exercises all of the powers of the different branches of government. The solution for Congress is to reintroduce a concept that Americans adopted more than two centuries ago: separation of powers.

The Natural Experiment of the Telecommunications Act of 1996

The FCC has combined the powers of all branches of government since it was formed in 1934. For much of the twentieth century, Congress and the communications sector were dissatisfied with communications law. The usual assumption was that it needed to be updated from its 1930s origins. That is precisely what Congress did in 1996, without removing any of the FCC's combined powers of government. Indeed, the Act gave the agency even greater powers.

The Act is a natural experiment to determine whether separation of powers matter, at least as manifested in the implementation of a new law. If the Act resolves the symptoms of concentration of powers—imprecise rules, regulatory uncertainty, appearance of arbitrary and discriminatory decisions, and an absence of discipline exerted by other branches of government—it means that separation of powers does not matter in the implementation of a new law in an isolated agency such as the FCC. But if those symptoms persist even under a new law, the separation of powers matters.

Under those circumstances, the concentration of legislative, executive, and judicial powers enjoyed by the FCC makes it unlikely to follow any law strictly. Regardless of what Congress, the administration, or even the courts may say, an agency with a combination of powers can write its own rules, enforce them as it sees fit, and adjudicate disputes under them. Under these conditions, there is little reason to expect dramatic changes as the result of a new law.

Of course, all large governmental bureaucracies, with or without separation of powers, are notoriously inefficient and often suspected of being unresponsive to political will. How can one distinguish the specific ill-effects of combining the powers of government in one agency from the general inefficiency of a government agency? A possible test is the reaction of the agency to a major new law that substantially redirects it.

An agency with separation of powers would implement a new law carefully, so as to avoid provoking the wrath of one of the other branches of government. An executive branch agency, for example, would seek to avoid being overturned in court. To avoid political criticism, such an agency would be expected to implement a new law without discrimination and, at least by its own standards, carefully and efficiently. This agency might still have the inefficiencies of a large bureaucracy, but it would be attentive to the details that would otherwise prompt harsh disciplinary action from the other branches of government.

In contrast, an agency without separation of powers would be little constrained by the other branches of government and would be less inclined to implement a new law carefully and efficiently. It would have little incentive for precision in rulemaking, clarity, efficiency, certainty, and nondiscrimination in both administration and adjudication.

This book draws on many examples from my tenure as one of five commissioners on the Federal Communications Commission from 1997 to 2001. Some of these examples directly relate to the implementation of the Telecommunications Act of 1996, and some pertain to the implementation of preexisting provisions under the Communications Act of 1934. In either case, the implementation at a commission with the combined powers of government was problematic. The 1996 Act failed to remedy the structural problems of the FCC as an administrative agency, even though the agency's failures to implement rules under preexisting laws highlighted those problems.

By examining the FCC's implementations of both communications laws, this book finds that the commission suffered under the effects of the combined powers of government. The problem was not that the Act was tough to follow; the problem was that the FCC was not structured to follow it precisely.

Structure of the Book

Chapter 1 presents the problems posed by the combination of the powers of government and the dashed expectations of the implementation of the

Telecommunications Act of 1996. Chapter 2 reviews the ancestry of the FCC under the Communications Act of 1934 with its combination of the powers of government. Chapter 3 describes the Telecommunications Act of 1996 and how it left the combined powers of government in place. Chapters 4 through 6 review the inability of different institutions (the courts, the administration, Congress, and the public) to effectively discipline the FCC, an agency operating with combined powers of government. Chapters 7 through 9 describe the results of the combined powers of government at the FCC: sloppy rules, regulatory uncertainty, and occasional discriminatory administration. Chapter 10 presents a case study of how the combined powers of government interfere with decision-making at the FCC.

1

Separation of Powers and Dashed Expectations

Expectations were high for the Telecommunications Act of 1996. In the mid-1990s, the communications sector was heralded as the new frontier.[1] America eagerly anticipated the Internet, wireless and satellite communications, digital television, and a host of other new technologies that would make science fiction seem short on imagination. Many believed that the only obstacles to a wonderful future were antiquated laws, particularly the Communications Act of 1934, which governed how businesses conducted themselves in the communications sector. For decades the FCC had been writing rules only tenuously related to the 1934 Act; it needed updating.

To overcome the obstacles, Congress passed the Telecommunications Act of 1996. The Act had many purposes, among them to allow practically anyone to offer communications and other services where regulators had long forbidden competition. Unfortunately, the Act preserved the FCC's multiple and conflicting responsibilities, including the writing of rules to implement it, the enforcement of those rules, and the adjudication of the disputes that would arise under them.

The FCC did not implement the Act precisely or without discrimination. Dissatisfied parties appealed the FCC decisions, and within a few years of the Act's passage, courts began to reverse them at a high rate. Investors who leapt into the communications sector after initial FCC rules were promulgated were dismayed to discover those rules overturned and constantly changing.

The reason for the investors' dashed expectations was that, regardless of the policy predilections of Congress, the FCC is an institution poorly structured to implement new laws because it combines all of the powers of government. Until Congress decides to restructure the agency with separation of powers, such policy prescriptions as the Telecommunications Act of 1996 may well go unheeded, or worse, be implemented through sloppy rules, enforcements, and adjudications, many of which will not withstand court scrutiny.

History of the Separation of Powers

As every schoolchild is taught, our federal government has separation of powers. Our government is divided into three branches: legislative, executive, and judicial. Each has effective checks or balances against the others. Thus, Congress cannot administer the laws it writes, but must rely on the executive branch for administration. Moreover, Congress must trust the judiciary not merely to adjudicate disputes under those laws, but also to compel a reluctant administration to administer and enforce even those laws it finds objectionable. The public can show its displeasure with Congress not merely by voting legislators out of office, but by asking to have the executive administer and enforce laws in a certain way regardless of congressional directions, or by seeking relief in courts from the excesses of Congress. In these and other ways, the executive and judicial branches provide counterweights to Congress.[2]

Similarly, the executive branch cannot write the laws it administers, nor fund its own operations, nor decide ultimately the constitutionality and legality of its actions. It depends on Congress for both statutes and funding, and it depends on the courts to uphold its executive decisions. A dissatisfied public can ask Congress to scrutinize, or even to withhold funding from, an executive branch agency. Or an individual can seek review of administration actions and relief from courts. Congress and the judiciary have the power to prevent excesses by the executive.

The judiciary cannot write the laws it reviews, nor can it fund its own operations or appoint its own judges. It depends on Congress for funding and statutes, and for confirmation of judges, who are appointed by the executive. A dissatisfied Congress can withhold funding from the judiciary or impeach individual judges or create new courts.

Our federal structure of separation of powers has been imitated not only by state and local governments in the United States, but by governments around the world.

European political philosophers of the seventeenth and eighteenth centuries emphasized the importance of the separation of powers partly as a reaction to the absolute monarchies of the time and the relative powerlessness of individuals. The usual epithet applied to the combined powers of government was "tyranny." The seeds of democratic government and individual liberty would not grow, or so the philosophers reckoned, under circumstances where the individual faced the combined powers of government embodied in any one institution.

From Cromwell's rebellion through the Restoration of the British monarchy, English writers, including John Locke, emphasized the separation of the executive and legislative functions of government. In the early eighteenth century, Montesquieu added the importance of a separate judiciary, and with it three branches of government, again in reaction to feeble judiciaries controlled by powerful monarchies.

The great innovation of the United States in the late eighteenth century was not its becoming the first democracy or the first republic; it was neither. Madison and Hamilton lamented the limitations of the republics of the time. It was, however, perhaps the first government consciously structured to have three balanced branches along the lines of Montesquieu and Locke, within the framework of a representative democracy. Separation of powers in our federal government was neither an accident nor the product of purely abstract reasoning. James Madison and the other framers of the Constitution witnessed excesses of British colonial governors and the British military during colonial times. Colonial governors, appointed by the government in London, would ignore the laws passed by locally elected colonial legislatures. During the ten years leading up to the War of Independence, the government in London, without colonial representation, imposed a series of taxes on the colonies. The military operated with abandon in the colonies, taking property and occupying houses at will. To respond to all of the excesses of British rule, the colonists found neither control in their local legislatures nor a method of appeal to a court.

Separation of powers was a prerequisite of any American constitution, not a contentious topic.[3] John Adams and others wrote about it in the years leading up to the American Revolution.[4] And while Madison and Hamilton did not believe in the fundamental goodness of all of those who served in government, they did believe that the self-interest of different factions within one branch of government, or between different branches, would prevent one group or individual from gaining excessive power. Louis Brandeis, dissenting in *Myers v. United States*, notes that

> The doctrine of the separation of powers was adopted by the convention of 1787 not to promote efficiency but to preclude the exercise of arbitrary power. The purpose was not to avoid friction, but, by means of the inevitable friction incident to the distribution of the governmental powers among three departments, to save the people from autocracy.[5]

The *Federalist Papers* are replete with discussions of the limitations placed on the powers of the government by the other branches.[6] Indeed, one of the stronger arguments raised by the antifederalists against the Constitution was that it did not separate powers sufficiently.[7] The response was that neither experience nor the influential writings of Montesquieu required absolute separation of powers.

Early American writings on government focused on three conditions painfully absent under British colonial rule: democratic control of government, preservation of civil liberties, and a structure of government to accommodate the first two. More than two centuries ago, government structure, including the separation of powers, was widely believed to affect democratic control and preservation of civil liberties. The manner in which laws would be written, enforced, and adjudicated depended on the structure of government. But the discussion of separation of powers during the founding of the Republic focused on the *entire* government, not on *individual agencies* within the government.

The Other Benefits of Separation of Powers

Separation of powers, then, both limits and balances powers in such a way that no branch of government or individual in the government has unlimited power. Preventing excesses of power regardless of intent is an enormous and well-known benefit of the separation of powers. Later in this chapter, the importance of checks and balances is described in more detail. But there are least three other lesser-known benefits of separation of powers not directly tied to limitations on the excesses of governmental power: the rule of law; reinforcement of democratic institutions; and efficiency of governmental services.

The Rule of Law. The powers of Congress or any legislature ultimately are to write laws and to provide funding for the administration of those laws. Those powers are dissipated if laws are not administered as intended, or if funds are not expended as authorized. Congressional powers also are wasted if courts are unwilling to find new statutes lawful or constitutional, or to adjudicate disputes under them.

Congress can enhance its powers by writing laws that are popular, easily administered, and capable of withstanding judicial scrutiny. The legislature will write more precise and less ambiguous laws, knowing that it cannot administer and adjudicate them. It must depend on its own precision in writing to influence the executive to administer laws as intended, and for the judiciary to adjudicate them as intended. In turn, if its laws are not followed, the legislature fears that the electorate will turn against it for ineffectiveness.

It is common for legislators to ask the executive branch about the difficulty of administering the provisions of a bill under consideration, or to seek legal counsel about how best to write a bill so as to withstand judicial review. Under separation of powers, the rule of law upholds legislative authority.

Similarly, executive powers erode if Congress withholds funding, or if the judicial branch reverses executive decisions. The executive can enhance its power by administering laws in such a way as to secure funding from Congress and to withstand judicial review. The rule of law consequently enhances executive power under separation of powers.

Not surprisingly, the rule of law enhances judicial power as well. Both Congress and the executive depend on the judiciary to uphold the rule of law. The rule of law rests on the foundation of an independent judiciary as the arbiter of disputes. If the judiciary is not independent, or if its decisions are not determinative in resolving disputes, there is no rule of law.

A well-functioning independent judiciary with the rule of law ensures a balance between the aspirations of both Congress and the executive.

Reinforcement of Democratic Institutions. The Constitution mentions public participation in influencing government in only a few instances: elections, the initial ratification of the Constitution, and amendments to the Constitution. Federal elections occur biennially, constitutional amendments less frequently.

Yet public influence over federal governmental behavior is constant, and much of that influence is exerted by individuals seeking the help of one branch of government to counterbalance perceived bad decisions by another. The separation of powers provides a means for the public to discipline each branch of government by bringing disputes to the others, and it increases the likelihood that public views are heard by government. Each branch recognizes, and fears, popular appeal to the others. Unjust, unreasonable, or undemocratic decisions are less likely to survive with separation of powers than without it.

The Efficiency of Governmental Services. The separation of powers helps ensure that each branch of government performs its functions more efficiently than it might otherwise. Thus, Congress, knowing that a disaffected public can appeal to both the executive and the judiciary, writes laws more clearly and more expeditiously and more precisely following public sentiment than it otherwise would. Knowing that the public can appeal unconstitutional laws to the courts, Congress is less likely to write unconstitutional laws. Knowing that the executive will try to misconstrue its legislative language, Congress provides oversight of new laws.

Similarly, separation of powers leads the executive to administer laws precisely, predictably, efficiently, and without discrimination to ensure that an independent judiciary will not otherwise reverse its administrative decisions, and that the legislature will continue to fund its programs. The executive, like the legislature, is fearful that the electorate will turn against it if it is ineffective. Fearful of complaints to Congress or appeals to the judiciary, it will administer and enforce laws more expeditiously and with less discrimination than it might otherwise. This is not to say that executive agencies are profoundly efficient; merely that they are likely to be more efficient than they would be in the absence of separation of powers.

The judiciary also handles cases more efficiently and with less discrimination than it might without separation of powers. An independent judiciary will be careful to rule precisely, knowing that legislature and executive could take steps against it if it acts arbitrarily and in a nonjudicial manner.

Isolated Agencies without Separation of Powers

It is likely that few Americans today ever consider the issue of concentration of powers in one branch of government. For most who have thought about it, the problem was solved in the Constitution. We need never worry about it again.

That assessment is accurate for our government as a whole, but not for discrete parts. The problems that result from a combination of powers are common to independent agencies such as the FCC, the Securities and Exchange Commission (SEC), and many others at the federal, state, and local levels. Some independent agencies, such as the International Trade Commission, do not exhibit concentration of power to the same degree because they are primarily adjudicatory in nature.

Concentrations of power, however, can also be found in such executive branch agencies as the Environmental Protection Agency (EPA), the Internal Revenue Service (IRS), and the Food and Drug Administration (FDA). The primary distinction between these and the so-called independent agencies appears to be that the president can remove the heads of the EPA, IRS, and FDA but may not replace independent agency commissioners at will. Government agencies with combined powers are less efficient, less responsive, and—as in the case of the FCC's failure to implement faithfully the Telecommunications Act of 1996—less accountable than agencies structured with a regard for the separation of powers principle.

Another distinction is that many agencies with combined powers of government have technical expertise. For example, the Food and Drug Administration writes rules for pharmaceutical products, enforces those rules, and adjudicates disputes under them. Congress does not frequently change the laws governing the FDA. Because the subject matter requires substantial technical expertise, courts are wary about second-guessing the agency. More disturbing, because the FDA entirely controls the commercial fate of its regulated businesses, the businesses are understandably reluctant to challenge its decisions in court. The agency faces remarkably little litigation.

Thus, we have examples of the combined powers of government in isolated agencies, within the framework of a larger government characterized by three branches, each primarily exercising only one of the three powers of government. Do these isolated examples matter to our overall system of government? Or did we sufficiently separate powers in our constitution so as not to be troubled by isolated deviations?

A Charmed Life

Scrutiny of agencies with combined powers of government has largely been limited to the independent agencies. They live a charmed life.[8] As an intellectual matter, the debate over the constitutional status of independent agencies has never been fully engaged, and yet the agencies have unequivocally won.[9] More than a century after the passage of the Interstate Commerce Act of 1887 and dozens of independent agencies later, no one seriously expects the agencies will ever be found constitutionally compromised. Few, if any, serious observers of the federal government suggest that these agencies are likely to recede in the next century. From a novel governmental institution in the nineteenth century, independent agencies became the bureaucratic structure of choice during the New Deal, when their number mushroomed.

The constitutional branches of the federal government tend to leave the independent agencies alone. Since the nineteenth century, the courts have sanctioned them, have given them enormous power, and have largely left them alone. Frustrated by ambiguous laws and content to let Congress delegate its legislative authority, courts allow the independent agencies enormous discretion.[10] Congress tends to like the concept of independent agencies as ostensibly independent of the administration and, thus, more under its own direction. Congress funds them and then leaves them alone, except for an occasional hearing to tell them how better to exercise legislative authority in writing rules. Various administrations appoint regulators but then ignore the agencies' autonomous exercise of administrative and enforcement powers. And the states occasionally—only occasionally—dispute them.

When one hears a claim that a government agency such as the FCC sometimes acts outside the law or is unresponsive to popular will, it is difficult to feign surprise. This view of extralegal agency behavior is not based entirely on either the jaundiced opinion of ideology or a cynicism encrusted on unending empirical evidence. The opinion that something very wrong would have the opportunity to grow from an agency that combines all three elements of government animated the debates over the U.S. Constitution.

Separation of Powers Matters, Even in Isolated Agencies

In this book, I suggest that separation of powers matters even in isolated agencies of the federal government. Of course, the consequences of isolated combinations of power in individual agencies are not catastrophic. Our broader governmental system of checks and balances means that the consequences of imperfections in one agency do not necessarily have far-reaching consequences throughout the government. The consequences of the absence of separation of powers in one agency can, however, be concentrated in the areas of law directly under the jurisdiction of that agency. Thus, lack of separation of powers for food and drug laws can have concentrated effects in the food and drug industries. Lack of separation of powers for environmental laws can have concentrated effects in the administration of environmental laws. As we shall see in this book, lack of separation of powers for communications laws can have a concentrated effect in the communications sector.

The efficiency and democratic influence of government gained by separation of powers are diminished in those agencies without it. Thus, an agency that combines all of the powers of government is less likely to write precise rules, less likely to administer rules efficiently or without discrimination, and less likely to adjudicate rules precisely or without discrimination. An agency that administers the rules it enforces is less likely to be concerned about writing precise rules because it can compensate for any imprecision through enforcement actions. Similarly, such an agency can compensate for bad administrative decisions through its adjudication process.

An appeal of an unjust, unreasonable, or undemocratic decision is more difficult in an agency that combines the powers of government than in an agency with separation of powers. Of course, within the framework of the entire federal government, countervailing forces preserve some efficiency and some democratic influence even on agencies without separation of powers. But agencies that combine the powers of government can be expected to be unresponsive and inefficient.

At the FCC, combination of powers did not begin with the Telecommunications Act of 1996. As we shall see in the next chapter, the FCC has combined all of the powers of government since its inception in the 1930s.

2

The Ancestry of the FCC

Most Americans probably harbor a sense that governmental actions are, or at least should be, based on specific legal authority. Thus, the traffic police officer monitors the speed of motorists relative to a posted speed limit, not relative to what the police officer personally believes the speed limit ought to be. In turn, the posted speed limit is stated on a sign erected by a local government employee in a location and with a posted speed determined by the local government, not by the employee. In every instance in which there is a governmental action, there is ultimately a specific law authorizing that action.[1]

Parties dissatisfied with these rules can and do appeal them to the agency promulgating them, or to a court of law. Disputes about whether a motorist has actually violated the speeding law are resolved not by the police officer, but by a duly appointed local traffic court. Similarly, disputes about whether an individual has violated a federal law are usually resolved in a federal court. A party unhappy with a rule promulgated by an agency, or an opinion letter it has issued, can usually challenge the rule through administrative law procedures.

For the higher tiers of law, the making of law, its administration, and the resolution of disputes are often handled by different agencies in respect of the separation of powers. The Federal Communications Commission, however, as an independent agency under the Communications Act of 1934, combines all three roles of legislature, executive, and judiciary. It acts as lawmaker, law enforcer, judge, and jury—all at the same time.

Expansive Power under the Communications Act of 1934

The Communications Act of 1934 created the FCC during the height of the New Deal and vested it with the powers of all three branches of government from the outset. In 1934, public concern about such concepts as separation of powers and government infringement on private property rights was at its nadir. Many assumed that private markets had gone wrong, and government needed all the power it could muster to fix them. While many if not most of the agencies created in the early 1930s had, by 1996, long since been abolished or radically changed in structure, the Federal Communications Commission survived largely intact.

The 1934 act gave the FCC extraordinary rulemaking authority throughout. Section 1 gave it the authority to "execute and enforce" all of the provisions of the act, including those that called for rulemaking or adjudication.

The FCC was not merely an enforcement agency, though. It would make decisions affecting specific parties—a form of adjudication—ranging from license applications, waivers, license transfers, and many other issues of interest to individual parties. The FCC also handled disputes, particularly between regulated licensees and other parties. The commission became a parallel court system, as described, for example, in section 207:

> Any person claiming to be damaged by any common carrier subject to the provisions of this Act may either make complaint to the Commission as hereinafter provided for, or may bring suit for the recovery of the damages for which such common carrier may be liable under the provisions of this Act, in any district court of the United States of competent jurisdiction; but such person shall not have the right to pursue both such remedies.[2]

The FCC's original responsibilities were to regulate one large telephone monopoly (AT&T), an oligopoly of large broadcast radio networks, and local radio stations. These were seen as presenting large problems even in the 1930s, requiring a large, full-time staff to write rules, enforce the same rules, and adjudicate disputes under them.

The FCC was given legal authority for specific responsibilities and broader authority for general responsibilities of doing good. For example, section 4(i) from the original 1934 Act gives the FCC extraordinary latitude with respect to "execution of its functions":

The Commission may perform any and all acts, make such rules
and regulations, and issue such orders, not inconsistent with
this Act, as may be necessary in the execution of its functions.[3]

A precise list of these "functions" is never given by statute. Similarly,
section 201 gives the FCC broad authority to act in the "public interest":

The Commission may prescribe such rules and regulations as
may be necessary in the public interest to carry out the provisions of this Act.[4]

Once again, the "public interest" is often invoked, but never defined, in
law. Section 303 also says that

except as otherwise provided in this Act, the Commission from
time to time, as public convenience, interest, or necessity
requires shall . . . make such rules and regulations and prescribe
such restrictions and conditions, not inconsistent with law, as
may be necessary to carry out the provisions of this Act.[5]

The "public convenience, interest, [and] necessity" are not defined in
statute, either.

Based on these expansive sections of statute alone, it is difficult to imagine what actions the commission might take, short of breaking another federal law, that the Communications Act of 1934 would not permit. Giving a
government agency license to do as it pleases was a dangerous prescription.
Courts were reluctant to limit the authority of the FCC.[6] Under these circumstances, the remarkable result is not that the FCC went beyond the narrowest interpretations of the statute, but how infrequently it engaged in
such adventurism.

Concentration of Powers and the FCC

The staff and commissioners who ran the FCC after its inception were capable and honest individuals. The tendency to promulgate rules outside the

narrowest construction of the law was not the result of either ambition or dereliction; the law seemed to give them latitude, which they chose to exercise. Once latitude has been exercised by a government agency, it is difficult to explain to Congress or expectant regulated entities why it will not be exercised again.

The expansive authority of the Communications Act of 1934 never instructed the FCC to separate its different powers or functions of government, and the agency never did. The infinitely elastic "public interest" and "public interest, convenience, [and] necessity" expanded the FCC's responsibilities in all areas, including rulemaking, enforcement, and adjudication. If the responsibilities of the different branches of government happened to be conflated, the Communications Act of 1934 did not object.

Despite ample opportunities to expand the scope of regulation outside the communications sector, the FCC rarely chose to do so. A "tyranny," the predicted outcome of the concentration of powers that might emerge from a reading of the *Federalist Papers* or any source concerned strictly with limiting the excesses of power, probably is not an apt description of the FCC. Whether through self-restraint, or mindful of the restraining powers of Congress and the courts, the FCC never attempted to exercise unlimited power throughout the economy.

But the other, lesser-known symptoms of the concentration of powers introduced in the previous chapter have characterized the FCC: less than full concern for the rule of law; less than full concern for democratic institutions; and less than full concern for the efficiency of government. If the FCC wrote a rule that an individual considered to be improper, the commission would be the first place to go to appeal the rule—or its administration, its enforcement, its adjudication, its reconsideration, or practically anything to do with it. At least in the first instance, the FCC sat in judgment of itself. Needless to say, the FCC could not detach itself to perform the different roles of government without being aware that it had performed all of the roles itself.

Of course, Congress could and did review the agency and its funding from time to time. Usually, the agency grew. Eventually, courts could and did consider complaints about FCC actions; but even after the elapse of substantial review periods, they were reluctant to get involved with seemingly technical decisions.[7]

The FCC Evolves over Time

When the Communications Act of 1934 was written, technology and communications markets were much simpler. Telephone service was viewed as a luxury, not a necessity. Millions of American households had no phone service. Telegraphy was a major industry. Radio was a popular and widely available medium for information and entertainment, but radio receivers were costly luxuries. Television was not commercially available, and wireless services were largely the province of the military and the infant aviation industry. The original language of the Communications Act reflected the technology and industry of the time.

With each passing decade, new communications technologies became available, and the FCC gained many more responsibilities and problems to resolve. For example, Congress gave the FCC new responsibilities with respect to broadcast television in the 1940s and '50s, and with respect to satellite communications in the 1960s. The Communications Act of 1934 was amended every few years to reflect advances in technology.

Congress was relatively prompt to recognize these new technologies, but it never significantly tampered with the structure of the FCC. It also never saw fit to give the FCC narrower responsibilities than the public interest, or to instruct the FCC to separate the different powers of government.

At the beginning of the 1970s, the FCC still primarily regulated a few identifiable large firms—AT&T, NBC, CBS, ABC—and thousands of smaller telecommunications and broadcast firms. For all of the agency's potential failings, the structure of regulation had become relatively predictable. The FCC regulated businesses that were not fully exposed to all manner of competition, making moderate requests with which they would comply in order to keep their licenses.

Unlike the idealized balanced governments of Locke and Montesquieu, the FCC was not self-correcting. If it made a mistake in a rulemaking, the same individuals who made the mistake would enforce the rule and adjudicate it. Mistakes lingered and translated into imprecise rules and inefficient administration and adjudication. The whole system worked as long as the FCC dealt with a relatively small number of regulated entities, each of which was willing to play along with the regulation game rather than fight it. When the FCC was challenged in court, it sometimes lost. Without full-blown competition, the closed system of regulation did not reveal the inefficiencies of some firms being forced to make a few more concessions than others.

Within a decade, however, the number of regulated technologies and firms exploded. Cable television and commercial satellite services gained widespread popularity, along with commercial mobile radio and other wireless services. The familiar, first-name basis for FCC regulation came to an end.

Congress Considers Revising the Communications Act of 1934

Beginning in the 1970s, Congress held hearings on the need to revise substantially the Communications Act of 1934, and with it the FCC. The primary motivation was the AT&T monopoly, and the question whether a more competitive telecommunications industry might benefit the economy.

The issue was not *whether* to change the Communications Act of 1934, but *how* to change it. Efforts to rewrite the law began as early as the Ninety-fourth Congress in the mid-1970s, with a bill introduced in the House of Representatives by Teno Roncalio of Wyoming. In 1976, hearings began in the House Communications Subcommittee under the chairmanship of Lionel Van Deerlin of California.[8] During the deliberations on the telecommunications reform legislation in the 1970s–90s, speakers demanding retention of the status quo at the FCC were hard to find.

Even so, for the next two decades, every major effort to change the Communications Act of 1934 failed. Yet dissatisfaction with the 1934 Act grew rather than abated. The problems facing the FCC also grew. By the mid-1990s, the growth of new technologies and new firms that had begun as a trickle in the 1970s turned into a torrent. Congress was aware that the Communications Act of 1934 was written during a different, simpler epoch of technology. This had led to anachronisms, such as prohibitions on companies entering new lines of business.

These prohibitions were inefficient. For decades, American corporations entered and exited businesses as opportunities developed. Thus, General Motors sold cars to consumers and tanks to the Department of Defense. General Electric sold refrigerators to consumers and specialized parts to aircraft manufacturers. But the flexibility to enter a new line of business, or even to leave an existing one, was not available to many FCC licensees. Thus, a broadcaster could not, according to the FCC, own a newspaper. And a telephone company could not offer cable service. Consistent with the Communications Act of 1934, the FCC pigeon-holed companies by establishing rules of what they could or could not do based on the parentage of the licensees, and individuals both inside and outside the affected industries saw these rules as retarding new commercial services and offerings.

State regulators placed additional restrictions on regulated businesses entering new lines of business and on new entrants competing against protected, regulated businesses, particularly telephone companies. These state regulations potentially conflicted with federal policy, and one of the purposes of revising the Communications Act of 1934 was to coordinate better regulation at the federal and state levels, particularly for telecommunications services.

But the issues faced by the FCC were not limited merely to the translation of old laws to apply to new technologies, or the coordination of federal and state actions. By the 1990s, a sample of concerns inadequately addressed by prevailing communications law included:

- the consent decree problem;

- the unending bureaucracy problem;

- the technology retardation problem;

- the antitrust problem;

- the false scarcity problem;

- the cost-accounting problem;

- the cable problem; and

- the "public interest" problem.

The Consent Decree Problem. The largest American corporation for much of the twentieth century was American Telephone and Telegraph, later called simply AT&T. It owned most of the local telephone systems in communities around America and most of the long-distance assets in the country. Until it was forced to divest itself of Western Electric, it owned the primary manufacturer of telecommunications equipment. It owned Bell Laboratories, the primary research facility for telecommunications. And, in the eyes of many, for much of the century it strongly influenced the government agencies charged with regulating it at both federal and state levels. In motion pictures, television, and other forms of popular culture AT&T, or "Ma Bell," came to symbolize a ubiquitous presence, at times thought of as efficient, at times thought of as omnipresent and malevolent, burdened with every conceivable form of caricature for both good and ill.

The close relationship between AT&T and the government was not accidental. The government had set up much of the monopoly, prohibiting competition in the early part of the twentieth century. AT&T and "the phone company" were synonymous.

Despite government involvement, beginning in the second half of the twentieth century AT&T was involved in a series of antitrust lawsuits.[9] To end protracted litigation, in 1982 it entered with the Department of Justice into a consent decree, under whose terms it divested itself into eight companies: seven regional companies with local service assets such as switches, copper loops, and local customers; and the remaining assets—including long-distance services, international services, equipment manufacturing, and Bell Laboratories—under a company retaining the AT&T brand name. The divestiture was completed in 1984.[10]

While the divestiture is sometimes hailed as one of the most visible manifestations of federal antitrust law in the twentieth century, the greatest effect of the consent decree may well have been that major decisions in telecommunications markets were now made by a single judge rather than by groups of regulators. In neither case were decisions made by private firms reacting to consumer interests through the mechanism of markets. Under the AT&T consent decree, the divested companies remained under rigid control of the court—Judge Harold Greene's Federal District Court— that had approved the consent decree.

Curiously, Judge Greene's consent decree suffered from a combination of powers even more than the FCC. Judge Greene's court took on the powers of approving rules, enforcement actions, and adjudications—all of the powers of government embodied in one person! For twelve years, little of significance happened in the telecommunications world without the approval of Judge Greene, and an entire legal bar developed for the specialized practice before his court.[11] The result, not surprisingly, was a diminution of the rule of law, a decline in public participation in governmental decisions affecting the communications sector, and inefficient decision-making.

The regulation of an entire industry by one judge under a consent decree was clearly unstable and unsustainable. Aside from the specialized bar that practiced before Judge Greene, no one much cared for this process. The consent decree was a general document that left out many details for the operation and governance of the divested companies. Judge Greene filled in the details. Even so, many issues remained unresolved, leading either to a need for clarification or disputes between companies. Petitions involving many large corporations with tens of billions of dollars in assets all came to Judge Greene's court. Resolutions might take months or years.

Because Judge Greene alone established the precedents, he alone could break them, and sometimes he did. For businesses, getting permission in Judge Greene's court was a convoluted and expensive game. Business decisions were delayed pending his decisions. Yet the consent decree process could only be ended by the court monitoring it, and Judge Greene seemed in no hurry to do that.

The process could not go on forever, if for no other reason than that Judge Greene was not a young man. One of the motivating factors for the Act of 1996 was a need for Congress to find a successor to the unstable consent decree.

The Unending Bureaucracy Problem. Like any administrative agency, the FCC was not known for speedy service. Indeed, many industry observers complained that the agency was unusually slow to write and enforce rules and resolve disputes. For example, the commission began a proceeding in the early 1980s on the "Fairness Doctrine" governing the editorial content of broadcast programming. By 1996, after several FCC rulemakings and several court challenges, the rules had not been resolved. The Fairness Doctrine (discussed in more detail in chapter 4, below) became a well-known example of the unfairness that results from an absence of expeditious decision-making.

The inefficiency of the FCC was compounded by the combination of the powers of government. Generally, individuals dissatisfied with the inefficiency of an administrative bureaucracy in the executive branch can go to the legislative branch and complain about poor performance, or go to the judicial branch and seek to compel action from the executive branch. These remedies are not as easily available for dealing with an independent agency such as the FCC.

Administrative delays, of course, are rarely spiteful or malevolent. In an agency with a wide array of responsibilities, some administrative functions take a lower priority. Individuals can and do complain to Congress about slowness of FCC administrative processes, but complaints from Congress often have limited influence at the agency. Similarly, courts are reluctant to compel the FCC to act on administrative matters if the complaining party has not exhausted all available administrative remedies at the commission. Needless to say, exhausting those remedies can take a long time when the same agency that caused the delay is responsible for reviewing complaints about it.

The Technology Retardation Problem. Another motivation for reform was the desire to remove barriers to product and service innovation. The first application for FM radio service was submitted in 1934. Although the service was soon introduced, decades of regulatory interference limited its further development. It took a full generation for FM to develop into the pervasive and flourishing format it is today.[12] The first cable television systems were developed in the early 1950s. For the next thirty years, the FCC succeeded in retarding the development of cable television by putting restrictions on the programming cable operators could offer their customers.[13] The first cellular telephone application was in the 1950s; the first licenses were delayed until the 1980s.[14] The first applications for ultra-wideband technologies for spectrum languished for more than a decade. The value to both consumers and businesses lost by delayed deployment of these technologies is inestimable.

Once again, the combination of powers at the FCC played a role in technological retardation. Applicants for licenses for new technologies appealed bitterly to both courts and Congress. The response, appropriately enough, was that they must exhaust administrative remedies at the FCC.

Doubtlessly, many more applicants were exhausted before administrative remedies were. If a separate agency had nothing beyond licensing responsibilities, it might have handled applications more transparently and expeditiously, or at least enabled an applicant to exhaust administrative remedies expeditiously.

The Antitrust Problem. The United States has often been likened to a consumer's paradise. If you want to buy anything, you can probably buy it in America. A cart of groceries, the grocery store, a chain of grocery stores—anything can be bought in America. The government imposes a few effective limitations on consumer purchases such as drugs and alcohol. For businesses, it also limits purchases that may upset the competitive conditions of a market. Thus, antitrust laws preclude a business or individual from acquisitions that would result in an unlawful level of market power. Consequently, all acquisitions of businesses of any significant size are automatically subject to Hart-Scott-Rodino antitrust review.[15] Antitrust laws and the antitrust authority of the Department of Justice (DOJ) and the Federal Trade Commission (FTC) are codified in statute.

Before the 1996 Telecommunications Act, the FCC could rely on no clear statutory instruction to write ownership rules other than vague "public interest" language. An acquisition of any size in any industry would be reviewed by the Department of Justice or the Federal Trade Commission, the competent statutory agencies responsible for administering federal antitrust law. The FCC, perhaps having doubts about the efficacy of these federal agencies, or wanting to replicate their work, or preferring a new means of imposing its own policy designs, took upon itself the task of reviewing acquisitions in the communications sector.

Ironically, the FTC and DOJ go to great lengths to avoid reviewing the same case, both to conserve resources and to prevent a form of double jeopardy under federal antitrust law. Yet the FCC has long engaged in this duplicative process—wasting resources and subjecting private parties to a form of double jeopardy—partly in order to encourage private industry to fulfill the agency's own policy agenda.

Duplication of antitrust acquisition review was rarely a problem before the 1980s, because most large firms regulated by the FCC were unlikely to merge with one another. This changed with the explosion of technologies and greater competition in the communications sector in the '80s, which also led to more such mergers.

As we shall see in chapter 9, separation of powers might have led the FCC to avoid reviewing mergers in detail or engaging in ad hoc means to select cases for review. It might also have led to more expeditious reviews and more efficient use of resources, rather than wasting them on rules that duplicate the efforts of others. And separation of powers could also have led to a greater sense that governmental decisions with respect to mergers and acquisitions in the communications sector were based on a rule of law rather than a rule of available power.

The False Scarcity Problem. In the decades before the Telecommunications Act of 1996, FCC rules regarding transactions were sometimes arbitrary. Without reliance on economics or antitrust principles, the FCC established caps on the number of certain types of licenses an individual or entity could own. The limitations did not apply to all licenses. There were, for example, no limitations on the ownership of amateur licenses or point-to-point microwave licenses in a market. There were, however, limitations on broadcast licenses. A broadcaster could only own one television station or a very small number of radio stations in any given market, and a finite number of stations overall nationwide. These ownership caps were not based on empirical studies or clearly reasoned judgments. They were literally plucked out of thin air. The courts were not amused.[16]

The limitations applied not just narrowly to the holding of broadcast licenses. Broadcasters were restricted as to ownership of newspapers and cable outlets as well. From the 1950s through the early 1990s, they faced restrictions on ownership interests in program production and even syndication rights under the Financial Interest and Syndication Rules. They were also restricted in the types and ownership of programming they could air during certain hours of the day under the Prime Time Access Rules.

Virtually all of the rules affecting broadcasters were rationalized with the assumption that spectrum—that is, the distribution of wavelengths and frequencies—was scarce, and that broadcasters did not face effective competition. The combination of these two suppositions enabled the commission to write practically any rules it saw fit—or so opined the Supreme Court in *Red Lion Broadcasting Company v. FCC* in the late 1960s.[17]

The underlying foundation of *Red Lion* seems profoundly naïve, if not by the standards of knowledge of the 1960s, then surely by the market realities of the twenty-first century. The *Red Lion* court based its decision on the following syllogism: Spectrum is scarce; spectrum is valuable to distributing speech; the FCC regulates spectrum; therefore, the FCC may limit speech. *Red Lion* failed to recognize that much of spectrum "scarcity" in the 1960s was the direct result of restrictive FCC rules. The Supreme Court effectively rewarded the poor regulatory performance of the FCC with respect to spectrum with the additional opportunity to limit speech in America.

Yet the rules based on scarcity of spectrum were less likely to have been written, much less survived for decades, if federal communications policy had been subject to separation of powers. An agency responsible only for writing rules would likely have been more deferential to statutory language, where scarcity is not mentioned. Even if rules based on scarcity were written, entities harmed by such rules would likely have been more eager to appeal them if the rulemaking body were subject to separation of powers.

The Cost-Accounting Problem. In the sixty years of the Communications Act leading up to 1996, it is almost certain that the FCC never engaged in a serious exercise to estimate fully the costs of a single regulation, much less the costs of all regulations. Ignoring costs was not unique to the FCC; it was and remains the standard government practice of regulation.[18] If the commission had had to account fully for the costs of its rules, it might have had a more difficult time engaging in the wars against various industries, as described below.[19]

Once rules were written, they stayed on the books in perpetuity, whether they had outlived their usefulness or not. In 1998, substantial rules related to telegraphy were still on the books.[20] Rules that might have been written for one purpose would ultimately serve other purposes with the passage of time.[21] The FCC had no mechanism to remove outdated or unnecessary rules from the books.

The Cable Problem. Of all the major industries in America in the early 1990s, one of the easiest targets for a politician to bash was cable television. Americans in increasing numbers loved to watch cable, and by 1992, the majority of U.S. households subscribed to it. Paradoxically, as prices rose and professional comedians introduced more jokes about the poor quality of service, more consumers signed up. Despite the jokes, poor quality, and rising prices, American consumers viewed cable subscription as a good value relative to other uses of their money. Nevertheless, Congress identified the cable television industry as a target prime for attack.

And attack Congress did. It passed the Cable Act of 1992, sponsored by Representative Ed Markey and others, in the middle of September.[22] The Cable Act of 1992 was a substantial amendment to the Communications Act of 1934, subjecting the cable industry to the severest forms of FCC regulation for the first time. The bill would impose price regulation, and practically every other form of regulation known to government, on an industry that had largely been unregulated since 1986.

The industry, confident of a presidential veto, did little lobbying to soften the sharpest edges of proposed statutory language. Some observers believe that industry leaders such as John Malone had inflamed congressional passions against cable. In any event, the first President Bush obligingly vetoed the bill. As evidence of just how unpopular the cable industry already was (and how unpopular President Bush had become in the last months of his presidency), Congress overrode the veto on October 5, 1992, presenting Bush with his first veto override.[23] This was a severe blow to the cable industry.

The FCC was given substantial latitude in the implementation of the law. It had the authority to write detailed rules, administer them, and adjudicate disputes under them. The result was that the FCC did not always keep to the narrowest interpretation of the law, nor did it write predictable rules expeditiously.

Under Chairman James Quello in 1993, the FCC ordered a reduction of approximately 10 percent in cable rates based on a simple but robust economic model called a benchmark model. This was apparently not enough for Chairman Quello's successor, Reed Hundt, who demanded larger reductions. In 1994, the FCC reduced cable rates by an additional 15 percent.[24] To justify a foregone conclusion, FCC economists examined endless numbers of possible models until one was found to yield the predetermined outcome. It was an unfortunate use of talented economists and the economic discipline for political purposes. Without separation of powers at the FCC, the result was political excesses, because neither consumers nor businesses could effectively and expeditiously appeal unreasonable FCC decisions to other branches of government. U.S. cable investment dollars simply headed elsewhere for more hospitable investment climates.[25]

The "Public Interest" Problem. Many of the technologies and market situations encountered by the FCC after 1934 were not specifically addressed in the Communications Act of 1934. The FCC had two choices to address issues arising under circumstances not specifically addressed under law: It could wait for Congress to decide how to write laws to address these novel circumstances, or it could assume authority under the vague "public interest" language found throughout the Communications Act of 1934. An imaginative FCC could read the public interest language to give it the authority to write rules as necessary, to enforce those rules as necessary, and to adjudicate disputes as necessary. In essence, under the "public interest" doctrine, the commission had all the authority it would ever need to address any problem imaginable, and it no longer needed Congress to write new laws for it. Throughout much of its history, the FCC has been a staunch advocate of the "public interest" doctrine.

The "public interest" doctrine became a means for the FCC to expand its rulemaking, administrative, and adjudicative authority at will. Not only had Congress granted the FCC all of the powers of government; it even gave it the authority to fill in missing gaps of authority. The law was viewed as so elastic that it could cover any conceivable action by the commission.

All of the attendant problems of the combination of powers were exacerbated by the "public interest" standard. The rule of law was undermined because the FCC could write rules as it chose, regardless of specific statutory language, with less fear of reversal in court than would otherwise be the case. Similarly, the FCC would attempt to stretch the public interest standard to its administration of rules and its adjudication of disputes under them. Democratic institutions were subsequently undermined because the public found both Congress and the courts reluctant to interfere with the FCC and its public interest standard. If the FCC were slow and inefficient to administer some provisions of law, there was little adverse result for the agency.

Subtle Problems

The problems associated with the combination of powers under the Communications Act of 1934 as described in this chapter did not result in tyrannical rule. But the combination of powers *did* have deleterious effects on the body politic nonetheless: erosion of the rule of law, weakening of democratic accountability, and a serious loss of governmental (and economic) efficiency. These subtle, even insidious, evils resulted from the structure of the FCC.

It would be an exaggeration to claim that the combination of powers at the FCC created a crisis in government, a conspicuous mishandling of public activity. Government of the FCC's form could function with a combination of powers, but not well; and by the mid-1990s, the problems reviewed in this chapter afflicted government regulation of the communications sector. Each had two potential types of solutions. One was to write statutory language instructing the FCC to reach a different regulatory outcome. The other was to restructure the FCC so that it no longer would be legislator, policeman, judge, and jury, all in one. The disinfecting power of public scrutiny in agencies subject to separation of powers might have been enough to produce substantially improved regulatory results. As we shall see in the following chapter, Congress, largely in response to industry suggestions, chose the former approach.

3

The Telecommunications
Act of 1996

For twenty years beginning in the mid-1970s, Congress continually attempted to revise the Communications Act of 1934. Each successive Congress came closer but ultimately failed, until the 104th Congress in 1995–96.

Legislation that takes twenty years of gestation naturally breeds skepticism that it will ever pass. When Congress finally passed the Telecommunications Act of 1996, the vote was overwhelming in both houses with only a few dissenters, and reflected cooperation among majority and minority party leadership, including Republican representative Tom Bliley of Virginia and Democrat John Dingell of Michigan, and senators Larry Pressler, a Republican from South Dakota, and Fritz Hollings, a Democrat from South Carolina.

The 1996 Telecommunications Act was passed in part because practically all of the different sectors of the communications industry were exasperated with the status quo of communications law. No one knew what the future would hold, but it seemed that almost any change was better than the prevailing situation at the FCC.

Solutions

In its creation of the Telecommunications Act of 1996, Congress carefully attempted to address most, if not all, of the issues presented by industry, including the problems listed in the preceding chapter. Their solutions might be seen as follows:

- *The consent decree problem.* The Telecommunications Act of 1996 terminated the 1982 consent decree that settled the 1974 AT&T antitrust case and placed the FCC largely in charge of residual obligations of the Bell Operating Companies. The FCC was assigned the responsibility of writing rules, in part superseding state authority, to open local telecommunications markets to competition.

- *The unending bureaucracy problem.* In an effort to avoid perpetual rulemakings, Congress placed timelines on most new regulatory responsibilities of the FCC and attempted to limit the discretion of the commission in many of its proceedings by providing detailed instructions. For example, the local market-opening provisions of the Act were designed to give the FCC less rather than more discretion. Sections 10 and 11 of the Act placed time-lines on the FCC to review its rules.

- *The technology retardation problem.* Congress inserted language into the law to promote innovation of new services, both in the preface and in specific sections of the Act, such as sections 10, 11, and 706.

- *The antitrust problem.* The House Judiciary Committee reviewed the Telecommunications Act of 1996 and removed the FCC's limited antitrust jurisdiction. Some thought this removal would end much of the merger review process at the FCC, but the agency would continue this practice under its license transfer review process.

- *The false scarcity problem.* Congress relaxed some of the restrictions on broadcast ownership.

- *The cost-accounting problem.* Congress required the FCC to review its rules every two years under sections 11 and 202 and remove those that no longer made sense.

- *The cable problem.* Congress rewrote many of the cable provisions of the Communications Act, giving far more flexibility to the cable industry and removing most forms of price regulation.

- *The "public interest" problem.* Congress did not specifically address the "public interest" problem. Indeed, Congress added the phrase many times to new statutory language. Perhaps it thought that the FCC, with enough specific new instructions, would not need to rely on the "public interest" standard.

- *The combination of powers problem.* Congress did not address this problem.

February 8, 1996

On February 8, 1996, chief executive officers, major politicians, and the media crowded the Great Reading Room of the Library of Congress, one of the grandest rooms in all of Washington. President Clinton, with Vice President Al Gore and actress Lily Tomlin looking on, signed the Telecommunications Act of 1996. Outside, limousine drivers were making more than a good day's pay taking dignitaries to and from this hard-to-reach spot. An invitation to the signing ceremony was a hot ticket.

People who had fought one another—and would continue to fight one another for years—gathered together to say nice things about one another. Rarely have so many people been gathered in one place, each convinced that he or she knew something that no one else in the room fully appreciated—the particular phrasing of one section of the bill or another, or the mergers and acquisitions that were planned after the signing, and the fortunes that would be made.

Successful business ventures are richly rewarded in part because most new ventures fail. Sophisticated businessmen know the odds are long. That day, however, everyone was smiling, each assuming that he would be the successful survivor. Practically everyone that day thought the Telecommunications Act of 1996 was an enormous success that would be good for business. Surely the problems that had vexed the communications industry had been solved by the Act.

Ironically, that day few people had actually read the Act in its entirety. It was available online on the Thomas search engine at the Library of Congress Web site. But Washington and much of the world still expected paper copies, which were rare as of that date, though summaries by dozens of experts were readily available.

How would a company plan business based on a much celebrated, but largely unknown, law? And how could one develop a business plan in February of 1996 when detailed regulations with the force of law would not be written for months?

Everyone felt the excitement of competition—not of competition on the edge of victory, but competition on the edge of beginning a long race. If only it were clear what the rules of the race would be. No one knew. Surely the first few months would hold the worst of the uncertainty. Within six months, the Federal Communications Commission would have written many of the most important rules. Within a little more than a year, all of the rules would be written. Of all of the different views that day of the future of the communications sector, few could have been based on an ever-growing FCC and unending court defeats. Surely, after years of close combat, the war to win the communications sector would move from Washington to Wall Street and Main Street.

There were perhaps five hundred people at the Library of Congress on February 8, 1996. Each of them was convinced that the Telecommunications Act of 1996 would be good for the communications industry and good for America. All of them were convinced they knew what the Act meant and how it would be interpreted. As would soon be apparent, few of them agreed on exactly what the new law meant.

A Triumph of Individuals over Government

In its simplest form, the Telecommunications Act of 1996 was intended to be a triumph of individual over government decision-making. Since the 1920s, federal and state governments had dictated practically every business decision made in communications and broadcasting services. For most forms of telecommunications, service was restricted to a single, regulated monopoly or a small group of closely regulated firms. For an existing company to change the quality or types of service offered, the government had to review all plans and make a decision on each detail. The process was tedious. It stifled innovation. Competition was prohibited. And the consumer was left defenseless, a pawn of government decisions.

Although various agencies limited competition in many industries in the first half of the twentieth century, by 1995 government effectively prohibited competition in only a few, such as postal service, electricity, and telecommunications. The Act addressed the communications sector. From then on, or so the law seemed to promise, the individual, not the government, would decide who would offer services, to whom, at what price, and with what features.

August 8, 1996. The Act gave the FCC many responsibilities to write new regulations, with firm dates for rules to be completed. Many of the first deadlines under the Act were six months after enactment, or August 8, 1996. By that date, much about the Act was more clearly recognized than at the time of enactment:

- Practically all issues raised and addressed by Congress were subject to rules to be written by the FCC. Implicitly, the Act gave the FCC enormous new authority and discretion.

- The Act did not diminish any of the FCC's responsibilities under any of the branches of government—legislative, executive, or judicial.

- The Act gave the FCC additional responsibilities in areas previously reserved for the states; the exact boundaries of those responsibilities would be determined only by years of litigation.

- Hundreds of new firms were rapidly being formed, and existing ones expeditiously reshaped, in anticipation of the new FCC rules.

- The eyes of much of the communications sector were focused on the FCC.

In August 1996, the FCC issued in a timely manner new rules required by the Act to instruct local telephone companies of their responsibilities to interconnect with other phone companies and of their obligations to lease equipment and services to competing companies. Over the next year, the FCC would issue many new orders implementing rules without precedent, all presented in hundreds of pages of new regulations. It would write new rules for spectrum auctions, as well as conduct several such auctions that would generate billions of dollars of new receipts for the U.S. Treasury. It would review a series of new major mergers in the communications sector, such as Bell Atlantic–NYNEX. The FCC was one of the busiest federal agencies at that time.

For the most part, all of this activity was looked upon with approval. There was grumbling, to be sure, about specific aspects of the Act and its implementation, but with market capitalization in the industry growing rapidly, the complaints were barely heard amidst the adulation. Between 1996 and the first quarter of 2000, the Act was the toast of the communications world.

No Branch of Government to Discipline the FCC. But the initial August 1996 orders also offered firm evidence to some government officials and business leaders that the FCC rulemakings might be headed in the wrong direction. State officials and incumbent local exchange carriers were particularly concerned that the agency reserved too much power and discretion for itself and not enough for state officials, despite years of careful negotiation with Congress of statutory language that was supposed to preserve their authority. Some members of Congress grumbled publicly about the new rules, and the Iowa Utilities Board and others initiated litigation challenging the FCC's interpretation of the Act.[1]

But no branch of government stood ready to limit the excesses or miscalculations of the FCC. The Clinton administration worked closely with the FCC and apparently approved its every move.[2] In *AT&T v. Iowa Utilities Board*, the Supreme Court gave the commission substantial latitude to write rules as it saw fit. Many members of Congress supported its general direction. Those who disliked that direction, or merely disapproved of the agency's tactics, felt powerless to stop it. The Telecommunications Act of 1996 had taken decades to pass Congress. Its passage had been at a singular moment in time and could not be readdressed soon. In the late 1990s, as it administered an Act that seemed to have solved problems that had long vexed the communications industry, the

FCC was an enormously powerful government agency. No branch of government appeared to stand in its way.

The Bubble Bursts

In January 2000, following four years in which hundreds of billions of dollars flowed into the communications sector, investors still thirsted for communications-related investments. Investor demand buoyed new stock offerings, and corporate bond issues were concentrated in the communications fields. Prices of telecommunications and related stocks had risen more than 300 percent in four years, much more rapidly than the broader market indexes.[3] Privately held firms added substantial value as well. Money managers almost universally looked at investments in the communications sector as being good as gold. The Telecommunications Act of 1996 was given credit for much of the new investment, and it was difficult to find a politician who was not taking credit for this market boom through his or her own efforts to pass the Act.

And then the bubble burst. Within months, the financial fabric of the communications sector began to unravel. The stocks that had been so quickly bid up based on exaggeration and hype went into freefall. The telecommunications industry alone quickly lost more than 90 percent of its peak market value. Many firms went into bankruptcy, including WorldCom, Global Crossing, and Adelphia.[4] Northpoint, PSINet, Teligent, Winstar, and others simply ceased to exist as independent companies. Many others came perilously close to bankruptcy. Businesses accused of creative accounting—WorldCom, Qwest, Global Crossing, Adelphia, Tyco, and even Enron—all had major telecommunications activities.

It was almost certainly the largest financial collapse of any one sector in American history. Investors and lenders, both large and small, were left to wonder at the rapid evaporation of trillions of dollars of value in their telecommunications investments.[5] Employees, once standing on the cutting edge of technology, were left standing in the unemployment line. And customers were left with the bad taste of unmet promises.

The losses spread rapidly. Manufacturing firms that had financed their telecommunications customers' expansion plans were left holding the bag.

The difficulties of companies such as Winstar became problems for vendors like Lucent that had sold equipment on credit to their credit-hungry, under-capitalized customers. The new telecommunications firms also owed large sums to incumbent carriers for connecting them to their customers.

A generation earlier, the vicissitudes of the financial markets were of direct concern primarily to the wealthy, but by the 1990s, interest in markets had permeated American society. Practically all American workers and retirees owned stock through pensions and retirement accounts, and they knew it. When the stock market rose in the 1990s, nearly everyone, from the secretary to the CEO, felt better off. When the stock market fell, everyone felt poorer. For the first time since 1987, Americans watched financial reports with a sense of anxiety and woe.

In no sector of the economy was the crisis of confidence greater than in telecommunications. No one knows exactly how much money was lost from the peak of the communications bubble in the first quarter of 2000 through the trough in the second half of 2002, but the blow was staggering.

The losses were not just financial. Hundreds of thousands of employees lost their jobs. Those who kept them were shaken by the decline in the industry, the loss of equity value, and the ever-shrinking possibility of accumulating wealth in the industry. Millions of individuals who had invested their careers in the communications sector now seemed destined for both uncertain and hard times.

In retrospect, it is difficult to understand why some warning signs had not been clearer. Telecommunications had always been a relatively small part of the economy, certainly no more than 2.5 percent, and the broader communications sector no more than 5.0 percent.[6] Why should it attract such a disproportionate share of new investment? In an economy estimated optimistically to grow at 3 or 4 percent a year, stock values in an entire sector cannot continue to increase at double-digit rates forever. But the same simple mathematical principles that fail to explain precisely the rise in the stock values also fail to explain the pattern of its fall.

The fall in the stock market was not entirely or even largely from the relatively small communications sector. But its collapse and the problems of individual companies in that sector were disproportionately large and unavoidably visible.

Causes of Boom and Bust

What caused the telecommunications bubble in the late 1990s? No one knows for sure. It was part of the larger phenomenon of stock market bubbles, but it had peculiarities of its own, and no single explanation seems convincingly to account for what happened.[7]

Benign Explanations. Many of the potential causes were hardly sinister. Economic expansion followed by contraction partly explains the timing of the bubble, although which was the cause and which the effect is not clear. Low interest rates in the late 1990s may have made debt more attractive than equity as a means of raising capital, but the debt-financing was hardly peculiar to the communications sector. Moreover, while broad macroeconomic factors may help interpret the movements of the broader market, they do little to explain the peculiarly exaggerated pattern of the communications sector.

For instance, in the past several decades, the opening to increased competition of many industries that were previously heavily regulated has attracted a flood of new entrants, which in turn might have bid prices to much lower and less profitable levels. This may help to account for some of the particular effects of the uncharted regulatory regime in the communications sector. But it does little to explain either why stock valuations initially surged from 1996 through 2000 and the timing of the decline, or why all firms suffered when specific regulatory policies should have hurt some and helped others.

We might also take note of the portion of the flood of new investment capital that found its way into the hands of management teams with little or no experience in telecommunications markets, or with poor business plans. But while markets predictably punish poor business plans, they must surely reward wise and prudent ones, and practically no companies in the telecommunications sector did well between 2000 and 2002. Poor management may have caused the particularly dismal fortune of a few companies, but it cannot account for the fate of the entire sector, nor can it explain either the timing or the pattern of stock valuation.

In the mid- and late-1990s, most market forecasts predicted substantial growth in Internet demand, particularly high-speed services, and accelerated use of the Internet as a mode of commerce. The direction of the forecasts—calling for increased demand—all proved true; but most forecasts were consistently too optimistic about the pace of change. Many businesses developed business plans around market forecasts that overestimated consumer demand for new technologies and new services. But bad Internet information should not have adversely affected companies that did not rely on Internet-related services for market demand; and surely investors with large sums at stake make investments based on more than the idle projections of forecasters. If erroneous forecasts of future demand can lead to false increases of value of certain securities, surely an individual investor with even the slightest degree of skepticism could have made a fortune either selling the market short or selling better information. Some savvy investors doubtlessly did well selling the market short, but the lack-of-information theory fails to explain why the skeptics were so substantially outgunned by the gullible lemmings.

Bad Behavior. Old-fashioned dishonesty clearly contributed in isolated instances to the roller-coaster ride. There is no shortage of examples. Conflicts of interest, for one, occurred as Wall Street investment analysts reported favorably on companies doing business with their financial institutions. This form of self-promotion, while perhaps not illegal at the time, might have confused some unwary investors. But while there may well have been many such conflicts in the investment analyst community, it was rarely if ever the case that only one analyst would report favorably on a stock while all other analysts reported negatively on the same stock. Moreover, conflicts were not limited to communications. Other sectors, such as health care and pharmaceuticals, doubtlessly had conflicts of interest for analysts, yet they did not experience the same collapse.

Blame for the collapse has also been directed toward the corporate CEOs, internal financial officers, and external auditors who were guilty of faulty accounting and bookkeeping. Officers of WorldCom, for example, were convicted of such wrongdoings. Some of these practices might have been used at first to create the appearance of financial growth that fueled the stock market, and others later might have been used to cover up poor investments in the aftermath of the market collapse. No doubt, many executives acted poorly and some even unlawfully.

It is difficult, however, to attribute entirely the expansion and collapse of the telecommunications sector to the unethical behavior of individuals in corporate America. Unethical behavior was not invented in just the past few years, nor is it plausible that it is more concentrated in one sector than others. Some other explanation is necessary to explain both the timing of the stock market expansion and collapse and its concentration in the communications sector.

Bad Implementation of a Law. It is the inadequacy of all these hypotheses that brings us to the Telecommunications Act of 1996 itself. Was the Act simply a mistake?

No one thought so in the heyday of the mid- and late-1990s, when corporate leaders never made a statement or speech about the communications sector without paying homage to it. After 2001, though, the Act increasingly became a target of blame for the collapse of the telecommunications industry. Perhaps, or so the logic goes, it needed to be scrapped, or at least rewritten. It is a convenient story, and has the advantage of not relying entirely on the newfound unscrupulous behavior of individuals to explain the rise and fall of the stock market from 1996 to 2002. But if the law was so bad, why did the stock market skyrocket for the first four years after its passage?

Here is a different explanation: The combination of powers at the FCC prevented an efficient and predictable implementation of the Act. Based on the rules for the sector initially written by the FCC under the Act, companies, both public and privately held, raised hundreds of billions of dollars and invested money in plant, equipment, and business development. These were sloppy rules that eventually would not hold up in court. Further, the FCC fostered an environment of regulatory uncertainty, and it occasionally engaged in discrimination against or in favor of individual companies.

Meanwhile, each branch of government assumed that the responsibility to rein in the FCC was more properly the domain of a different branch. Most private parties shied away from challenging the agency in court and saw little hope in complaining to either Congress or the administration; these political branches had no effective control or oversight of the day-to-day decisions of the FCC. Ultimately, years after the initial rules were written, courts did respond to a few brave legal challenges, and the FCC was as likely as not to lose. But with each loss, legal rights in the communications sector became less rather than more certain, and incentives to invest in the industry eroded. Investors once burned by rules reversed years later by courts were understandably reluctant to invest again in the sector.

These problems would now be of limited interest if the economy and the communications sector were still growing as rapidly as they did in the 1990s. A strong economy can make the public very forgiving of failures to implement the will of a democratically elected government. But the weakening of the economy from 2000 to 2002 and the collapse of the communications sector after 1999 only magnified the importance of the FCC's problems.

The Core of the Problem

What went wrong with the Telecommunications Act of 1996? Some suggest that the problems were simply personnel problems, and that getting the right team in place at the FCC would solve them. But the very notion that good government depends on having the "right" people smacks of elitism. It also begs the question: What happens when the "right" people leave? No two Americans, much less two major political parties, could possibly agree on the identity of the "right" people. We must look elsewhere for the core of the problem.

The 1996 Act changed much of the policy direction that was wrong with preexisting communications law—for instance, by removing formal barriers to market entry and ending certain forms of price regulation—but it left in place the powerful institutional structure of the FCC that combined the powers of all branches of government. In retrospect, it is unclear how well these changes could ever have been implemented in an institution without separation of powers.

Given its vast power, it is not entirely surprising that the FCC was reluctant to abandon power and was easily tempted to expand it. For example, the Act could have been taken as an opportunity either to expand or to contract the role of price regulation, one of the most destructive forms of regulating markets. Price regulation was not mandated in the Act, but neither was it prohibited. And yet, an Act with repeated and explicit references to deregulation was interpreted instead by the FCC as a mandate for the creation of new price regulatory schemes. In its vagueness, the Act implicitly gave the FCC substantial discretion to make such interpretations.

There is also a great deal wrong with the way the FCC does business. As a regulatory agency, it hears disagreements on practically every issue: competitive carriers disagree with incumbent carriers; broadcasters disagree with cable operators; satellite operators disagree with terrestrial wireless carriers; small companies disagree with large companies; and so it goes, with many different issues. From among these disparate views about policy *outcome* there emerges a remarkable consistency of views about *process* at the FCC. Below are some of the widely shared opinions of what the problems are:

- *A fuzzy reading of the law and sloppy rules.* The FCC all too often treats communications law, including the Act, selectively and inconsistently, losing litigation with alarming frequency. The incentives at the agency appear to encourage legal adventurism. While some businesses benefit from particular instances of fuzzy reading of the Act, practically all parties can point to instances where they believe they have been harmed.

- *Uncertain protection of rights.* Even where the FCC has followed the law, it has done so in a way that constantly postpones decisions and leaves the resolution of court defeats undecided and policy outcomes uncertain. The net effect is that parties before the FCC have little idea about the extent and contours of their rights either today or tomorrow. The natural response to uncertainty is delayed decision-making and a shunning of the sector by investors.

- *Discriminatory treatment.* A surprising number of parties before the commission believe that they are not treated the same as similarly situated parties. In major proceedings, the FCC will often have ad hoc processes that are not easily explained, much less replicated.

Perhaps most troubling is a widespread perception that the FCC is not self-correcting. There are no means of addressing these problems within the

FCC. Congress and the courts seem aware of many of them, but are unable or unwilling to force the FCC to address them.

None of these problems originated with the Act; each has a long history at the agency. Ironically, never having been implemented, the Act is nonetheless blamed for harms it could not have created. In recent years, many members of Congress were eager to introduce legislation to modify the Act to reach specific policy outcomes pertaining to broadband, spectrum, and broadcasting. Few, if any, of these legislative proposals addressed the underlying core issues of process that have long bedeviled the FCC.

The next several chapters examine in more detail the absence of discipline for the FCC.

4

The Courts and the Administration
Will Not Discipline the FCC

The potential of the FCC with its combined governmental authorities to exercise excess power would be curbed if one of the three major branches of the federal government would vigilantly review the agency and block its every excess. Under such circumstances, the FCC would be careful not to provoke that branch.

But which branch limits the FCC? As this chapter will explain, neither the executive nor the judiciary directly disciplines it. The absence of a substantial restraint can be seen in the implementation of the Telecommunications Act of 1996.

Since the day it was signed into law, the Act has been subject to questions about its meaning. While most of it is unambiguous, some words and phrases are vague, even self-contradictory. This may reflect legislative drafting designed to accommodate conflicting points of view, or it might simply be the product of an all-too-human process. Vagueness, ambiguity, and other shortcomings of statutory drafting afflict portions of all laws. The Communications Act of 1934 was, if anything, even less precise in its meaning.

The interpretation of the Act of 1996, as with that of 1934, has been largely up to the FCC, not Congress. Any intent that Congress may have had in writing a new law is easily lost when the agency interpreting it has both substantial discretion to interpret laws, pursuant to the so-called *Chevron* deference, and a combination of powers. Thus, we find that

- the Supreme Court holds that Congress, not courts, must discipline the FCC;

- the Supreme Court, in *AT&T v. Iowa Utilities Board*, sanctions FCC discretion as residual from the Communications Act of 1934;

- *Chevron* deference reinforces combined powers of government;

- despite the courts, the FCC limits speech;

- the administration will not interfere; and

- the FCC is left alone to divine congressional intent in writing the Telecommunications Act of 1996.

The Supreme Court Holds That Congress, Not Courts, Must Discipline the FCC

The exercise of wide discretion at the FCC did not begin with the Telecommunications Act of 1996. Practically all Supreme Court cases involving the FCC prior to 1996 pertained to the agency's exercise of delegated authority, usually legislative, not explicitly granted in the Communications Act of 1934. The Supreme Court usually let the FCC do as it pleased.

Prior to 1996, the Supreme Court had effectively endorsed expansion of the FCC's power, but it never sanctioned the commission for failure to perform its duties under the 1934 statute. The courts had found that the FCC in particular, among all federal agencies, had been granted extraordinary powers to exercise delegated legislative authority based on broad and vague language such as the "public convenience, interest, and necessity."[1] It was found to have authority to regulate technologies and markets that did not exist or could not even have been contemplated at the time of the passage of the 1934 Act.[2] It had been granted authority to regulate concepts not specifically found there, even authority to limit ownership of the rights to broadcast licenses, impinging on protected First Amendment speech.[3] The court-approved pre-eminent power of the FCC to exercise wide latitude in its decisions was enshrined long before the Telecommunications Act of 1996.

In perhaps the greatest expansion of the agency's powers, the Supreme Court relied on the judgment of the FCC rather than statutory principles in determining whether regulatory restraint was necessary.[4] In a 1940 ruling, Justice Felix Frankfurter may have summarized the view of the Supreme Court in expressing its desire to wash its hands of reviewing the many and varied decisions made by the FCC under delegated authority:

> Courts are not charged with general guardianship against all potential mischief in the complicated tasks of government. The present case makes timely the reminder that "legislatures are ultimate guardians of the liberties and welfare of the people in quite as great a degree as the courts." *Missouri, Kansas & Texas Ry. Co. v. May, 194 U.S. 267, 270, 24 S.Ct. 638, 639.* Congress which creates and sustains these agencies must be trusted to correct whatever defects experience may reveal. Interference by the courts is not conducive to the development of habits of responsibility in administrative agencies.[5]

Simply stated, Justice Frankfurter held that regulatory agencies were for Congress, not the courts, to discipline. He was implicitly saying that entities and individuals harmed by the FCC had little opportunity to redress those wrongs through the court system.

Sixty-five years later, Justice Frankfurter's words are remarkably current. The same words that offer little or no hope in legal remedies to individuals harmed by an administrative agency merely serve to embolden the agency.

Iowa Utilities Board Sanctions FCC Discretion as Residual from the Communications Act of 1934

From the outset of implementation of the Telecommunications Act of 1996, the FCC believed it had substantial discretion to interpret laws, even to promote specific social policies not directly found in statute. The Supreme Court gave a green light to this discretion in 1999 in *AT&T v. Iowa Utilities Board*, a case initially brought by state regulatory agencies and Bell Operating Companies against the FCC's interpretation of local competition rules under sections 251 and 252 of the Act.[6]

FCC Chairman Reed Hundt often spoke of the flexibility of the 1996 Act. He was at least partly right. It was vague in a few places, but certainly not as many as Chairman Hundt found or Justice Antonin Scalia, who wrote the decision in *Iowa Utilities Board*, suspected. The Act would never have become law otherwise. While Chairman Hundt viewed this occasional elasticity in statutory language as a virtue, Justice Scalia would describe the same characteristic as a flaw. He attacked the imprecision of the legislative language:

> It would be gross understatement to say that the Telecommunications Act of 1996 is not a model of clarity. It is in many important respects a model of ambiguity or indeed even self-contradiction. That is most unfortunate for a piece of legislation that profoundly affects a crucial segment of the economy worth tens of billions of dollars. The 1996 Act can be read to grant (borrowing a phrase from incumbent GTE) "most promiscuous rights" to the FCC vis-à-vis the state commissions and to competing carriers vis-à-vis the incumbents—and the Commission has chosen in some instances to read it that way. But Congress is well aware that the ambiguities it chooses to produce in a statute will be resolved by the implementing agency, see *Chevron v. NRDC*, 467 U.S., at 842–843.[7]

Justice Scalia's opinion gives broad discretion to the FCC, rather than the states, to write and implement rules. His opinion is not based so much on the Telecommunications Act of 1996—which he roundly criticizes—as it is on section 201 of the Communications Act of 1934, as amended in 1938, which escapes specific criticism. Section 201 is a grant of administrative and enforcement powers to what might otherwise be largely a rulemaking body—in essence, a grant of power combining different branches of government. By Justice Scalia's logic, the FCC did not need to wait for the 1996 Act to have the broad and vague authority to do whatever it wanted; that authority had been there for decades.

Justice Scalia's opinion, punctuated with a reference to *Chevron* (to be discussed in more detail below), is not the only plausible interpretation of the Act, but it is one that resolves a wide range of jurisdictional controversies in favor of the FCC. The Supreme Court does not address, nor was it asked to address, whether section 201 is limited to give the FCC authority only as "necessary"; nor does the Supreme Court address whether section 201 or the word "necessary" can plausibly be subject to the interpretation of the FCC alone.[8]

Justice Scalia had a choice between two sections of the 1934 Act—section 2(b),[9] which reserved powers for state governments, and section 201, which granted public interest authority to the FCC—that had peacefully coexisted for decades, but seemingly were at odds with each other with the advent of the 1996 Act.[10] Paradoxically, the House version of the Act, H.R. 1555, specifically addressed the issue by including all of the relevant new market-opening provisions as an exception to section 2(b).[11] Justice Scalia's opinion would have been unambiguously correct under H.R. 1555. But the language amending section 2 was dropped from the bill negotiated between the Senate and the House, creating the ambiguity and contradiction which the Supreme Court was left to resolve. Justice Scalia largely rendered section 2(b) meaningless.

In *Iowa Utilities Board*, the Supreme Court's decision was not that the FCC's rules were the *only* plausible interpretation of the law, but rather that the FCC actually had the *discretion* to interpret the law as it chose. The implication was that a future FCC could write yet different rules. The rule of law was reduced to what the FCC saw at any given moment in time.

Although the issue before the Supreme Court in *Iowa Utilities Board* was narrowly the rulemaking authority of the FCC, it would be difficult to interpret *discretion* for rulemaking without inferring discretion for enforcement and adjudication as well. Each of these is supported by the FCC rules granting itself authority to enforce rules and adjudicate them. *Iowa Utilities Board* did not limit the FCC's exercise of power from any of the three branches of government.[12]

Chevron Deference Reinforces Combined Powers of Government

In granting the FCC the authority to interpret the intent of Congress or the intent of a law, *Iowa Utilities Board* relies in part on the 1984 ruling in *Chevron v. Natural Resources Defense Council*, in which the Chevron

Corporation and others disputed the Environmental Protection Agency's interpretation of the Clean Air Act.[13]

The *Chevron* opinion, only a few pages long, uses the word "intent," or words with that root, sixteen times. It is a brief treatise on how administrative agencies should treat an issue not specifically addressed by law, and where congressional intent does not offer clear guidance for interpretation. Following *Chevron*, a law restricts the activity of an administrative agency only where the "intent of Congress" is precisely and unambiguously clear. Remove even a little precision or insert a little ambiguity, and an agency has substantial discretion:

> When a court reviews an agency's construction of the statute which it administers, it is confronted with two questions. First, always, is the question whether Congress has directly spoken to the precise question at issue. If the intent of Congress is clear, that is the end of the matter; for the court [467 U.S. 837, 843], as well as the agency, must give effect to the unambiguously expressed intent of Congress. If, however, the court determines Congress has not directly addressed the precise question at issue, the court does not simply impose its own construction on the statute, as would be necessary in the absence of an administrative interpretation. Rather, if the statute is silent or ambiguous with respect to the specific issue, the question for the court is whether the agency's answer is based on a permissible construction of the statute [footnotes omitted].[14]

This opinion has given rise to the so-called *Chevron* two-step test. The first step is to determine whether an issue is directly addressed in statutory language. The second step is to look to agency interpretation if the first step is not met: "Only if the statute is silent or ambiguous do we defer to the agency's interpretation, asking 'whether [it] is based on a permissible construction of the statute.'"[15]

As a practical matter, the need to address Congress's intention is impossible to avoid, given its inability when it writes legislation to foresee every potential "specific issue" that may arise in the future. This is particularly problematic for telecommunications law, which addresses a rather dynamic marketplace. Technological innovations periodically alter the landscape beyond recognition. Perhaps for that reason, *Chevron* does not instruct an agency to wait for specific statutory instruction, or even to construct the answer most consistent with existing statutory language.

Chevron suggests that Congress implicitly delegates rulemaking authority to the agencies, particularly technical agencies such as the FCC, for any number of potential reasons that the Court introduces with the adverb "perhaps":

> In these cases the Administrator's interpretation represents a reasonable accommodation of manifestly competing interests and is entitled to deference: the regulatory scheme is technical and complex, the agency considered the matter in a detailed and reasoned fashion, and the decision involves reconciling conflicting policies. Congress intended to accommodate both interests, but did not do so itself on the level of specificity presented by these cases. Perhaps that body consciously desired the Administrator to strike the balance at this level, thinking that those with great expertise and charged with responsibility for administering the provision would be in a better position to do so; perhaps it simply did not consider the question at this level; and perhaps Congress was unable to forge a coalition on either side of the question, and those on each side decided to take their chances with the scheme devised by the agency. For judicial purposes, it matters not which of these things occurred.[16]

The *Chevron* court also suggests that administrative agencies are equipped to decide on statutory ambiguities because the agencies are "political," inasmuch as the president is accountable to the people:

> An agency to which Congress has delegated policymaking responsibilities may, within the limits of that delegation, properly rely upon the incumbent administration's views of wise policy to inform its judgments. While agencies are not directly accountable to the people, the Chief Executive is, and it is entirely appropriate for this political branch of the Government

to make such policy choices—resolving the competing interests which Congress itself either inadvertently did not resolve, or intentionally left to be resolved by the [467 U.S. 837, 866] agency charged with the administration of the statute in light of everyday realities.[17]

But while the political structure of an executive branch agency such as the EPA is directly accountable to the president, the political structure of an independent agency such as the FCC is not. Once confirmed, FCC commissioners cannot be removed by the president. The *Chevron* court then opines that the judicial branch, precisely because it is not political (although perhaps no more nor less so than the FCC), is not in a position to choose among choices within the law:

When a challenge to an agency construction of a statutory provision, fairly conceptualized, really centers on the wisdom of the agency's policy, rather than whether it is a reasonable choice within a gap left open by Congress, the challenge must fail. In such a case, federal judges—who have no constituency—have a duty to respect legitimate policy choices made by those who do. The responsibilities for assessing the wisdom of such policy choices and resolving the struggle between competing views of the public interest are not judicial ones: "Our Constitution vests such responsibilities in the political branches."[18]

Chevron encourages agencies to test the boundaries of their rule-writing authority under the guise of reinforcing ambiguous laws. It is a virtual hunting license for ambitious agencies to find statutory ambiguities, or to invent them where none exist. In *Texas Public Utility Counsel et al. v. FCC*, the Fifth Circuit Court went even further, finding that a messy FCC interpretation of the statute for a federal universal service fund trumped one that was far clearer.[19] The 1996 Act established a federal universal service fund to support low-income individuals, high-cost telephone companies, rural health care, and schools and libraries. The 1996 Act, however, left the details of the fund to the FCC. In reviewing the FCC's decisions to implement the federal universal service fund, and in other areas, courts have chosen *Chevron* as an explanation for judicial passivity. *Chevron* has become little more than a sedative for courts clearly anguished by the imaginative excesses of agencies, but unsure of the proper role of the judiciary in reining in those excesses.

Chevron does not address shifts in the balance of powers when an administrative agency has wide latitude to interpret a law. Nor does *Chevron* address differences in the balance under different circumstances. For example, it is one matter to grant the Internal Revenue Service the authority to interpret statutes when there is an active and balancing court structure, Tax Court, to review IRS decisions promptly. It is a far different matter to grant the FCC the authority to interpret statutes when the first line of appeal of most FCC decisions is the FCC itself. The combination of powers at agencies such as the FCC and EPA means that the grant of additional authority under *Chevron* disrupts the balance of powers more than similar grants of authority to executive branch agencies with narrower powers.

Despite the Courts, the FCC Limits Speech

One court that has been particularly skeptical of the FCC is that which is most likely to review its decisions, the Circuit Court of Appeals of the District of Columbia.

A frequent observer of the FCC in court, Gene Kimmelman of the Consumers Union, once quipped: "There is such a fundamental hatred of [the FCC] in [the D.C. Circuit Court] that they can't trust them in any factual or policy determinations."[20] The mistrust this court has for the FCC is neither new nor partisan. Reputations are quickly acquired; bad reputations are slowly, if ever, lost. The mistrust is not without foundation; the FCC over the years has gone to great lengths to earn it.

How does a federal agency engender the mistrust of generations of judges of an entire court? The FCC accomplished this with its Fairness Doctrine, which was supposed to ensure balance in broadcast coverage of controversial issues.

Personal expression is one of the hallmarks of a free society, and this expression cannot be reviewed, much less censored, by the government. To some extent, any restriction on speech limits freedom. Of course, in most countries, there are well-recognized limitations on certain forms of speech, such as slander, libel, and indecent or incendiary speech. In many societies, including the United States, both political and commercial speech are less protected than individual speech.[21] The legal distinctions among different types of speech, and different levels of protection at the FCC, are as abstruse and refutable as are ecclesiastical distinctions about the number of angels on the head of a pin.

Except for some that may be imposed by the federal Food and Drug Administration, most limitations on commercial expression exist courtesy of the FCC. FCC rules impose limitations on broadcasting political statements[22] and on the definition of "educational" programming,[23] and specific restrictions in describing the federal universal service program to customers.[24] Indeed, in the late 1990s, the FCC compelled common carriers to describe the federal universal service program in terms that were less than truthful, and forbade carriers from disclosing universal service fees except under approved—often misleading—texts.[25] Unlike FDA rules, few FCC rules limiting commercial speech have been litigated in the courts. An exception is the so-called Fairness Doctrine.

Many cases could illustrate the judicial frustration with the FCC, but few rival the litigation surrounding various interpretations of personal attack and political editorial rules adopted by the Federal Communications Commission in 1967 as corollaries to the Fairness Doctrine. Time and again the court remanded the commission's rules with instructions to write, and justify, new ones. Time and again, the commission refused to cure the unlawful rules. Litigation continued for decades until the D.C. Circuit Court, in complete exasperation with the agency's delinquency, finally ordered the rules abolished in 2000.[26] By then, not one judge on the court or any commissioner on the FCC had served in office at the beginning of this litigation. The fault—and, in some circles, glory—did not belong to one individual. This was an institutional effort that spanned generations.

The Administration Will Not Interfere with the FCC

The *Chevron* opinion appears to countenance a substantial transfer of power from the legislative and judicial branches to the executive branch. Holding that the executive can find resolution among "competing interests" that the legislative branch cannot, *Chevron* grants it enormous rule-writing authority. Furthermore, the court says that executive branch decisions in these areas are beyond the grasp of judicial review.

The president cannot remove an FCC commissioner for any reason, even for voting the wrong way. Thus, even if an administration were inclined to discipline the FCC, it does not have the immediate power to do so. It can reward commissioners based on their behavior by offering renomination to the FCC or more desirable positions in the administration. It can threaten commissioners by refusing to renominate them if they seek renomination. But the ability of the administration to reward and punish independent agency commissioners is substantially less than its ability to do the same to its own executive branch officials. Those officials follow direct orders. Independent agency commissioners, rather like foreign officials, can negotiate with the administration at their leisure.

The FCC Is Left Alone to Divine Congressional Intent

Advocates of the exercise of wide FCC discretion in interpreting laws rely on a combination of *Chevron* deference and sections from the original Communications Act of 1934, particularly sections 1, 4, and 201. A series of court cases have interpreted these and other sections as giving the commission substantial latitude. Interpreted literally, they gave the commission all the power it needed long before the 1996 Act was written.

Perhaps it is true, as Justice Scalia suggests, that "Congress is well aware that . . . ambiguities in a statute will be resolved by the implementing agency." It does not follow, however, that Congress "chooses to produce" all of those ambiguities. Moreover, many, if not most, of the alleged ambiguities are not even in the 1996 Act.

Under *Iowa Utilities Board*, the FCC remained bound by strict limitations under administrative law even if communications law was no more bounded than the FCC's wildest imagination for the use of its "promiscuous rights." The opinion gave the FCC discretion, but the Supreme Court still held it to rational behavior, in accordance with administrative procedures. The D.C. Circuit Court of Appeals would eventually reverse subsequent FCC rules as inconsistent with the specific language of the Act.[27] Power was large under the Act, but it was not absolute.

Because of *Chevron*, however, there is interest in what Congress *intended* with the Telecommunications Act of 1996, in addition to the plain language of the statute itself. To obtain *Chevron* deference, an administrative agency need only demonstrate ambiguity in statutory language and intent. A simple search of the FCC Web site suggests that this is a common exercise; thousands of documents may be found referring both to "intent" and the "Telecommunications Act of 1996."[28] All too often, the divined intent is used to explain that the letter of the law should not be followed because it misses Congress's true purpose.

So what role *did* Congress intend for the FCC in interpreting its law? Doubtlessly little. Discussions of delegated authority and *Chevron* deference did not animate debate when the Act was written. When Congress writes statutory language, members may disagree about what it means, but they would hardly agree that it's unclear. The entire legislative process is rendered meaningless if agencies, particularly those outside any direct political control, have unlimited discretion to interpret the laws.

To understand the difficulty of determining precise congressional intent with respect to the Act, consider the motives of individual members of Congress, mostly unfamiliar with every detail of every piece of legislation they have to vote on. Factors playing at the individual level may be personal or partisan and have absolutely no bearing on "intent."

Looking to intent rather than actual statutory language ultimately increases ambiguity. The Telecommunications Act of 1996 merely amended the Communications Act of 1934, large parts of which remain intact. Whose intent matters? The members of the Congress of 1934? Or the members of each subsequent Congress that changed a few words here and there? Or the members of Congress in 1996? Or the members of Congress who again amended small parts of language in later years?

And if government comes to interpret laws based on intent rather than actual statutory language, why should legislators bother to write any statutes at all? Why not leave legal interpretation up to mind-readers specializing in intent? They will ignore statutory language, in any case.

The impossibility of determining the collective states of mind of thousands of legislators, both living and dead, suggests that greater fealty to the narrowest and clearest interpretation of statute language is the only practical path to proper implementation. When language is unclear, it should be left up to a future Congress to amend it.

What can positively be said about congressional intent with respect to the Telecommunications Act of 1996? It may be easier to frame the question in the negative: What could the Act not have meant?

Congress could not have intended to delegate to an agency such as the FCC the authority to rewrite the Telecommunications Act of 1996 or to ignore its specific provisions. Yet, on occasion, that appears to have happened. Whether it is interpreting telecommunications service to include computer equipment,[29] or interpreting "reciprocal compensation" to mean something other than what the statute says,[30] or interpreting "up to eight commercial radio stations"[31] as something else, or interpreting "shall review all regulations issued under this Act"[32] to mean "whatever," the commission has an unfortunate tendency to try to rewrite specific sections of the Act, all in the name of fulfilling congressional intent. In these and many other instances, the commission's rewriting is exactly wrong.

It is also doubtful that Congress could have intended permanent litigation and a failure to adopt final rules. As of 2003, for many sections of the Act, the commission had yet to adopt final rules capable of withstanding court scrutiny. What are the final rules for the property and contract rights of telecommunications carriers, whether incumbent or competitive carriers? No one knows.[33] And what process will be followed to reach final rules? An unending series of Notices of Proposed Rulemakings? No one who voted for the Telecommunications Act of 1996 could reasonably have intended these outcomes.

It is also unlikely that profoundly complex rules that require armies of lawyers to interpret them were the intent of the 1996 Act. The commission has ample discretion and responsibility under the Act. Exercising that discretion to construct complex sets of rules, where simpler rules or no rules might suffice, hardly seems the clearest interpretation of intent. Yet complex rules are exactly what the commission has wrought for telephony competition and for media ownership.

It is difficult to imagine that Congress intended the FCC to ignore costs of regulation. Yet the FCC indirectly imposes costs on interested parties through lengthy and complex proceedings, the use of economic cost models that require the hiring of experts to interpret, unending litigation, and profound uncertainty about the current and future states of regulation.

It is difficult to imagine that it was congressional intent to discriminate against certain industries or businesses under the Act, where the Act provides no such guidance. To anyone remotely familiar with its passage, the universal service section was written for small rural telephone companies, not to create new programs that would overshadow them. Yet the commission waited to deal with the small companies until after spending billions on schools, libraries, and large telephone companies. Commission apologists say that the little companies were given a hold-harmless provision. Operators of those companies would disagree with the proposition that they were not discriminated against by the commission in the implementation of universal service.

It is difficult to imagine that it was congressional intent under the 1996 Act for the commission to assume responsibilities of other government institutions while abandoning its own. Consider the FCC's interpretation of its responsibility to review its rules pertaining to media ownership once every two years. Between 1996 and 2002, the FCC reviewed its ownership rules only once, in 2000, rather than the statutory three times.[34] That review invented new approximations of competition standards—almost rudimentary in comparison to those used by federal antitrust agencies. Yet the FCC acts as if those federal antitrust agencies—equipped with their superior, non-FCC means of analysis—are incapable of protecting the public from abuses of market power.[35]

The Supreme Court in both *Iowa Utilities Board* and *Chevron* dumps the responsibility of disciplining wayward federal agencies squarely in the lap of Congress. The courts see this disciplinary responsibility as largely a political exercise, one for which the courts properly find themselves ill-suited. At least in the case of the FCC, as we will see in the following chapter, Congress is ill-suited as well.

5

Congress Will Not Discipline the FCC

Harry Truman once quipped that the "buck stops here"; the president cannot pass responsibility for problems to someone else. Truman obviously was not speaking about the FCC, because practically everyone associated with the agency looks to Congress, not the president, to solve its problems.

Although it may have the wherewithal to rein in the excesses of the commission, Congress rarely does more than send letters or hold hearings. There are various reasons Congress will not discipline the FCC:

- Congress is ill equipped to discipline the FCC.

- Congress has limited means to ensure that its intent is carried out.

- The FCC provides plausible deniability to Congress.

Congress Is Ill Equipped to Discipline the FCC

The suggestion that Congress is suited to promote "habits of responsibility" in agencies such as the FCC is no longer, if it ever was, accurate.[1] Congress is neither equipped nor inclined to discipline each and every misstep of any administrative agency. The congressional committees with direct jurisdiction over the FCC must, with small staffs, oversee dozens of federal agencies, of which the FCC is one of the smaller. The congressional committees have neither the resources nor the time to review more than a few highlights of FCC actions.

The congressional committees can and do hold oversight hearings of FCC activities. The hearings provide members of Congress with an opportunity to express their views directly to the FCC, and they are uncomfortable for commissioners or any FCC chairman out of step with congressional politics.

Many recent FCC commissioners, myself included, have come to the commission with experience as Capitol Hill staff members. This experience perhaps gives commissioners some insights into congressional politics and how to avoid serious political mistakes. But it does not give Congress additional leverage to influence FCC decisions. During my tenure on the commission, no member of Congress told me how to vote on any issue, much less asked me to change a vote. Congress can neither alter nor veto FCC decisions.

Congress does control the FCC's funding—the power of the purse. But except for a few rare cases in recent decades, it has substantially altered the budget authority of only a few agencies. Although the FCC could, in theory, be one of those few agencies subject to substantial review, in practice it is not. The authorization law for FCC appropriations can go for a decade or more without being renewed.

In recent years, practically all of the FCC's budget has come from the collection of "fees" on licensees rather than federal funds that require direct appropriations. Consequently, even if the FCC were to raise the ire of congressional appropriators, these Congress members would gain few federal funds to shift to other agencies by punishing the FCC. It is not an attractive target.

Congress Has Limited Means to Ensure That Its Intent Is Carried Out

A case that reveals much of the weakness of Congress in its oversight capacity of the FCC and its inability to ensure that its intent is carried out is that of the schools and libraries program.

As part of the broader universal service program, the 1996 Act instructs the FCC to provide subsidies for telecommunications services to schools and libraries. The Act does not speak of a separate schools and libraries program, much less one targeted at one set of schools more than another, much less a separately funded program, much less one funded at a specific level. All the law actually says is:

(B) EDUCATIONAL PROVIDERS AND LIBRARIES—All telecommunications carriers serving a geographic area shall, upon a bona fide request for any of its services that are within the definition of universal service under subsection (c)(3), provide such services to elementary schools, secondary schools, and libraries for educational purposes at rates less than the amounts charged for similar services to other parties. The discount shall be an amount that the Commission, with respect to interstate services, and the States, with respect to intrastate services, determine is appropriate and necessary to ensure affordable access to and use of such services by such entities. A telecommunications carrier providing service under this paragraph shall—

(i) have an amount equal to the amount of the discount treated as an offset to its obligation to contribute to the mechanisms to preserve and advance universal service, or

(ii) notwithstanding the provisions of subsection (e) of this section, receive reimbursement utilizing the support mechanisms to preserve and advance universal service.[2]

Consistent with the statute, the FCC could have set a discount of 0.1 percent for all telecommunications services to any school or library. But the FCC had other goals. From these words, the commission crafted a $2.25 billion program, aimed primarily at schools in low-income urban districts and at first largely targeted at providing equipment rather than services. It is impossible to read into the statutory language an intent remotely similar to the program the FCC invented.

Some critics of the implementation of the Act simply blame the sloppy statutory draftsmanship of Congress. The language of the Act in this subparagraph, however, was neither vague nor ambiguous. It did not lack specificity so much as it wanted a proper skepticism about the machinations of the FCC.

In late 1996 or early 1997, a senior FCC official visited the staff of the U.S. House of Representatives to better understand congressional intent on the schools and libraries program. Both Democratic and Republican staff gathered in a conference room in the Ford House Office Building to meet with the FCC staff.

The first question from the FCC staff sounded like it was from Mars: "Did Congress intend a $3 billion, or $10 billion, or $30 billion schools and libraries program under Section 254 for universal service?" All of the House staff looked at each other incredulously. "What is the schools and libraries program?"

In response, we were given the official FCC line about how to interpret section 254 on universal service, and commission staff pointed to the relevant subsection with its vaguest of references to schools and libraries. A senior staffer from the House Commerce Committee slowly and calmly explained: "I think that I speak for all of us on the House side, on both sides of the aisle. Under the Telecommunications Act of 1996, the House did not intend any radical change or expansion of the universal service program." No one on the House staff disagreed with him.

It was not just that the FCC was proposing a new program for universal service; the size of the program was truly staggering. Simple calculations show that a $1 billion program amounts to approximately $10 per year out of the pockets of every household—or much more than $3 for every person in America. How could anyone possibly read the Act to give the FCC the authority to set up such a vast, separate program, costing at least three billion dollars?

The FCC ultimately did create the program, despite the lack of any clear signal of intent from Congress, and scaled it at $2.25 billion annually. This was the result of a political compromise—not with Congress, but with the long-distance companies that ultimately would pay the multibillion-dollar bill. Congress held hearings, but the FCC suffered little more than momentary anxiety from the oversight.

The amount of funding had no specific congressional authority. The spending of any funds by an independent agency, much less $2.25 billion, without specific congressional authority is manipulation of the law. The FCC, by its own logic, had as much authority to spend $2.25 trillion as it had to spend $2.25 billion.

The beneficiaries of the schools and libraries program, unlike other universal service beneficiaries, were not part of the telecommunications network of the United States, the ostensible basis for the program. By collecting money from one group of users to subsidize service for an unrelated group of users, the program became an effective tax, and the most inefficient one imaginable.[3]

A few private companies initially challenged the program. One by one, they dropped their suits under pressure from the FCC. Ultimately, only GTE and some smaller companies retained their complaint against the government, and only on a narrow set of issues. In a peculiar opinion, the Fifth Circuit explained why the program was illegal but, in a few words, gave the FCC *Chevron* deference to interpret the law as the FCC, not the court, saw fit.[4] GTE, facing a merger review and other issues before the commission, did not pursue an obvious appeal. Many of the legal shortcomings of the schools and libraries program were never reviewed by a court.[5]

What happens when a government agency refuses to implement a law such as the Telecommunications Act of 1996 properly? As Hamilton described it in *Federalist Paper* 15, government is vested with the singular power to write laws, and that power is meaningless unless they can be enforced:

> Government implies the power of making laws. It is essential to the idea of a law, that it be attended with a sanction; or, in other words, a penalty or punishment for disobedience. If there be no penalty annexed to disobedience, the resolutions or commands which pretend to be laws will, in fact, amount to nothing more than advice or recommendation.[6]

When one branch of government refuses to implement a legitimate law properly, it not only disrupts the balance of the branches of government, it also becomes a tyranny unto itself, answerable to no one.[7] The choice of government activity reflects not popular sovereignty, but sovereignty of the government itself.

The details of the schools and libraries program are mind-boggling without any clear foundation in the statute. The Fifth Circuit Court recognized as much but took the path of least resistance—*Chevron* deference—even where the statutory language provided little basis for the program.[8]

The development of political support on Capitol Hill, for its part, was paradoxical. Table 5.1 shows the distribution by state on a per-capita basis of the roughly $2.1 billion in schools and libraries program funds that were actually allocated for the year 2000. While the exact pattern varied from year to year, some were fairly constant across all years: California and New York received more subscriber line funding both in the aggregate and on a per-capita basis than most other states; most rural states, the purported beneficiaries of section 254 and universal service, tended to receive far less than average, either on an aggregate or a per-capita basis.

Moreover, many of the most ardent supporters of a large schools and libraries program—the potential source of the "intent" for a large program—were from states that received relatively little from it. Thus, Senator Olympia Snowe from Maine and Senator John D. Rockefeller IV of West Virginia, who championed the program, were from states that received much less than 50 percent of the national average on a per-capita basis. This result remained true in most subsequent years. It is difficult to believe that this detail of the program was what either senator "intended."

Finally, table 5.1 shows a wide variation in expenditures per capita across different states. For every $1.00 spent in New Hampshire on a per-capita basis in 2000, more than $20.00 was spent in Puerto Rico. Tax collections per capita across the United States tend to vary remarkably little, so the per-capita contribution to the schools and libraries program is likely to have been close to $7.38 in each state. A casual glance at table 5.1 would suggest that if tax collections were equally efficient, and if there were no administrative costs for the program, residents of the forty states in the second two columns would have been better off supporting the schools and libraries program with state funds only, rather than accepting federal funds. But, as Jerry Hausman has observed, not all tax- or fee-collection mechanisms are the same, and the universal service fee structure is one of the most inefficient in the federal arsenal.[9] With a consumer welfare loss of more than two dollars for every dollar collected under this program, it is unlikely that citizens of many, if any, states benefit from the program.

It is difficult to reconcile this result with any plausible notion of congressional intent, or to trace the current schools and libraries program back to the Telecommunications Act of 1996. The program is based on an extremely aggressive interpretation of the Act. The fees that fund it are in all likelihood a tax,[10] and the Delaware corporation that administers it was created without lawful authority.[11]

TABLE 5.1

2000 PER-CAPITA EXPENDITURES ON THE SCHOOLS AND
LIBRARIES PROGRAM BY STATE

States receiving more than 150% of the national average of $7.38 per capita		States receiving between 100% and 150% of the national average of $7.38 per capita		States receiving between 50% and 100% of the national average of $7.38 per capita		States receiving less than 50% of the national average of $7.38 per capita	
Puerto Rico	$20.15	Mississippi	$10.69	Texas	$7.36	Maryland	$3.59
Alaska	19.08	New Mexico	10.21	Massachusetts	7.30	Nebraska	3.57
District of Columbia	16.43	Illinois	9.20	Connecticut	7.19	Minnesota	3.54
New York	14.51	Arizona	8.76	Oklahoma	7.09	Montana	3.46
California	13.92	Tennessee	8.18	Kentucky	6.49	North Carolina	3.40
Missouri	12.92			Arkansas	6.40	Florida	3.30
South Carolina	12.74			Georgia	5.87	Colorado	3.29
				Louisiana	5.70	Indiana	3.18
				Michigan	5.65	Washington	3.09
				Ohio	5.36	Oregon	3.06
				New Jersey	5.02	West Virginia	3.00
				Wisconsin	4.73	Kansas	2.88
				Pennsylvania	4.25	Vermont	2.74
				Alabama	4.21	Maine	2.70
				Rhode Island	4.10	North Dakota	2.68
						Virginia	2.61
						South Dakota	2.38
						Wyoming	2.28
						Utah	2.28
						Hawaii	2.13
						Idaho	2.05
						Nevada	2.02
						Iowa	1.80
						Delaware	1.78
						New Hampshire	1.00

SOURCES: Author's calculation based on information from the *2000 Annual Report of the Universal Service Administration Corporation*, appendix B; and U.S. Bureau of the Census, table 2, "Resident Population of the 50 States, the District of Columbia, and Puerto Rico: Census 2000," Internet release date, December 28, 2000, http://www.census.gov/population/cen2000/tab02.pdf (accessed October 13, 2005).

And, indeed, Congress was not too pleased with the final result. Both houses held hearings on the misdirected use of the universal service program in 1998.[12] Members in both parties expressed dissatisfaction with the schools and libraries program as being beyond the law and beyond congressional intent. But eventually the clamor died down. Over time, the political supporters of the schools and libraries program weighed in more forcefully than its opponents. Court challenges to the program were strongly discouraged by the commission, and the decision in the Fifth Circuit, though difficult to comprehend and transparently incorrect, was final.[13] Congress and business interests ultimately backed down, regardless of what the law said or what Congress had intended at the time of the passage of the Act.

The FCC Provides Plausible Deniability to Congress

The FCC has substantial political flexibility in situations such as that of the school and libraries program partly because it provides plausible deniability to Congress. For all of its potential shortcomings, the FCC, like other independent agencies, is not a political accident. The agency exists for many purposes and, by its very appearance of independence, serves the political purposes of both the executive and Congress.

The FCC makes difficult but necessary decisions involving complex and technical issues. Were Congress to make these decisions, disappointed parties would blame individual members for voting the wrong way. Similarly, were the administration to make these decisions, ire would inevitably be directed at it. When the FCC makes a decision, political anger at the administration and Congress is muted. They have plausible deniability of responsibility.

The interaction between Congress and the FCC is publicly visible and useful to Congress. Congress can hold public hearings and send forceful and publicly visible letters to the FCC. These public displays enable Congress to reflect and voice the concerns of constituents, even if the FCC ultimately decides against those concerns. Members of Congress can truthfully demonstrate to constituents their efforts, even if the results are negligible.

Of course, the president nominates FCC commissioners from both parties, and they are confirmed by the Senate. The nomination and confirmation process suggests political influence and even responsibility from both branches, but much can happen during a five-year term. Neither the administration nor Congress can use the commissioner selection process to micromanage every decision of the FCC. And, as we shall see in the next chapter, the public does not expect these branches of government to have such influence.

The FCC Cannot Discipline Itself

As this chapter and the previous one have revealed, none of the three branches of government is likely to discipline or balance the FCC, although each branch assumes that another will do so. It is unrealistic to assume that the FCC can discipline itself. It performs the functions of all three branches of government, which all require different and incompatible relationships with the public.

Rulemaking is naturally for legislators who have direct contact with the public and are cognizant of political concerns that govern the writing of laws. Those who make laws and rules cannot be shielded from hearing and weighing public concerns on a wide range of issues.

The judiciary has the opposite relationship with the public. Judges are shielded from the public. They hear only selected disputes, and they only weigh information related to those disputes, based on formal procedures. It is improper for judges to hear, much less consider, information on a wide range of issues in deliberating on the resolution of disputes.

The executive branch must administer and enforce rules with a delicate balance between vigilantly obtaining information on the one hand and impartially enforcing those rules on the other. Like the legislature, the executive must have unrestricted access to the public. Like the judge, the executive must administer rules impartially.

The commissioners and staff of the FCC have high professional and ethical standards. They are placed in an impossible position. Without losing control over the agency, they cannot simply divide it into three unrelated parts, one rulemaking, one executive, and one judicial. Some individual or group must be responsible for each of the parts of the FCC, and by statute that group is the FCC commissioners themselves.

The FCC commissioners cannot choose to adopt the behavior of one branch of government without compromising their responsibilities for another. They cannot behave like legislators with full access to the public without compromising their adjudication role. They cannot cloister themselves like judges without limiting their role as rulemakers. They cannot vigilantly collect information as an executive without influencing their position as judges. They cannot weigh the political concerns of legislators without reducing their roles as impartial administrators and adjudicators of law.

We have now come full circle in reviewing which branch of the federal government will discipline the FCC. The administration has little influence. The courts point to Congress. And, given its many other responsibilities, Congress offers little guidance, much less discipline, to the FCC. As we shall see in the following chapter, individuals outside of government are also unlikely to discipline the FCC.

6

Individuals Do Not or Cannot
Discipline the FCC

In our democracy, the various branches of government and the FCC itself are proxies for the public. Members of Congress, for example, as elected officials, reflect concerns expressed by their constituents. Concerns of private individuals and corporations are forcefully expressed to Congress about the decisions of the executive branch or the judiciary. Members of Congress are usually quite willing to express those concerns as a reflection of popular will. Individuals can also express their views directly to the administration and even to the judiciary. Surely the same reflection of democratic concerns must be true for the FCC, as well. Otherwise, the agency would be a political anomaly, entirely beyond the reach of political discipline for any real or perceived excesses.

Individuals, organizations, and businesses do, indeed, have many channels in our governmental and political system to express their dissatisfaction with a government agency, but despite the availability of democratic remedies, the FCC appears to be largely undisciplined. This result is clear in several areas to be explored in this chapter, including

- problems associated with insulation from the public;

- unresponsiveness to citizen concerns;

- the reluctance of individuals to take disputes to the FCC with its combined powers.

Problems Associated with Insulation from the Public

Studies of modern political economy are filled with examples of government bureaucracies failing to apply a predictable and narrow interpretation of the law. Political economists describe government behavior as subject to motivations and opportunities, not just the letter of the law. Their models explain that government may be unduly influenced by outside interest groups, and that regulatory enforcement authority may be captured and used to further agency power. They also explain how regulation is used as a tool by businesses to harm competitors, and how government agencies use regulatory authority to extract rents from private enterprise. Rather than seeing them as mechanical exercises beyond the control of any interested force of society, political economists describe government regulations as pieces used in a strategic game by groups or individuals pursuing their own interests.[1]

The opportunities for a government agency to engage in bureaucratic games increase when the agency incurs no cost for such behavior. The primary means to exact costs from it is the imposition of discipline and oversight from other government agencies and from the public. At its best, a government agency—fearful of offending the public with inferior service and of being replaced as a consequence—provides public services with as little market interference as possible. It often follows its statutory instructions narrowly, even if it has the opportunity to go beyond them.

The FCC in recent years has not always feared public reaction, either in its decisions or as a consequence of its poor performance. Seeming at times to view the law as an instrument of policy, it has been careless about following it and meeting public demands, and it has been willing to engage in activities clearly outside its jurisdiction.[2]

Federal agencies, including the Environmental Protection Agency, the Consumer Product Safety Commission, the Food and Drug Administration, the Occupational Safety and Health Administration, and the Central Intelligence Agency, are frequently accused of exceeding their mandates. Few have not suffered an embarrassing loss of a court challenge to their authority when they have strayed beyond the law. These violations, however, are thought to be the exception rather than the rule.

The FCC is not a renegade agency, a rogue that holds the law in utter contempt, always operating around it. Rather, it usually attempts to uphold the law. The FCC has, however, occasionally viewed the law as a means to pursue a political agenda, such as was described in great detail by a former chairman of the FCC in a 2000 book.[3] In those rare instances, the FCC decides on a policy and then works backwards to find a way for the law to support it, pursuing purposes and interests that transcend the law. If the public has no means to discipline the FCC directly, those occasional policy initiatives can go forward with little or no external restraining discipline.

Unresponsiveness to Citizen Concerns

The United States is a consumer-friendly country. One can purchase almost any imaginable item or service and find satisfaction where businesses compete to please customers. Those that annoy a customer do so at their peril. American consumers have perhaps more ways to vent their anger than those in any other country. They can complain directly to a company or take legal action against it, bring their problems to the attention of regulatory agencies or consumer advocacy groups, complain directly to politicians, or even take their complaints to competitors only too happy to help potential new customers give their rivals headaches.

For telecommunications matters, a consumer can complain directly to a member of Congress or the FCC, or both. Each year, the FCC receives thousands of complaints directly from the public, ranging from expressions of anger at rate increases by local phone or cable companies to outrage at the content carried by local broadcasters. Often, the FCC can legally do little about a specific complaint other than bring it to a company's attention. It is a tedious, thankless task, but answering public inquiries is an important role for government.

In 1997, the FCC had a large backlog of inquiries from congressional offices about many matters, including individual consumer complaints. Congressional offices had long grown accustomed to slow service from the FCC. Then chairman William Kennard, to his great credit, took these complaints seriously and assigned additional commission staff to the task of answering them.

Yet the mere fact that consumers in large numbers, dissatisfied with the provision of a private service, must resort to complaining to the government is a disturbing indicator of the failure of government regulation itself. A well-functioning market based on clearly defined property and contract rights should lead to the resolution of customer complaints by the sellers of services. Unfortunately, in the communications sector, competition is not allowed to be the source of discipline it should be to deliver consistently reliable service. Frustrated consumers, tired of complaining to unresponsive firms, turn their fury on a government agency that has all too often tinkered with the law to create at least some of the problems about which the public complains in the first place.

Because of the FCC's unresponsiveness to public concerns, Congress has become the primary sounding board for grievances regarding the commission. Offices of members of Congress and congressional committees frequently hear from the public about the FCC with a wide range of complaints: amateur radio licenses that have not been issued, lack of agency response to poor cable and satellite television services, problems associated with spectrum auctions, problems with telephone bills, and problems with programming on television and cable.

Congress is unlikely to discipline the FCC even when it is aware of problems affecting the public and private parties, however. Below are examples of cases in which Congress did not act on the public's behalf, and the public was either unwilling or not in a position to act on its own.

A Hidden Tax. An instance in which the FCC had little external discipline from Congress on behalf of the public is the case of "universal service," already discussed in the preceding chapter with reference to the schools and libraries program. In 1997, AT&T and other long-distance carriers entered into negotiations with the FCC after threatening to disclose to consumers universal service fees charged to them under the Telecommunications Act of 1996.[4] These fees went into the universal service fund, established at the bidding of Congress to replace roughly $2.5 billion in existing informal programs that had subsidized services for high-cost areas and low-income households. In addition, the fund was authorized to create new subsidy programs for telecommunications services to schools, libraries, and rural medical facilities.

The fund was to collect fees assessed on telecommunications carriers providing interstate services, principally the long-distance carriers such as AT&T, MCI, and Sprint. As with any fees assessed on competitive businesses, they would ultimately come out of the consumer's pocket. The Act required that these access fees be made explicit, presumably visible to consumers. But the FCC had grander ambitions for the universal service fund than Congress had mandated, involving new spending programs to be supported through these fees. Naturally, the agency did not want the fees to be visible to the American consumer, preferring instead a hidden tax, whose receipts it would be unconstrained to spend as it saw fit.

In the middle of 1997, the FCC announced that the universal service fund would be more than twice the size of existing programs, thanks to the new multibillion-dollar schools and libraries program, which was aimed at fulfilling the political agenda of the Clinton administration and visionary plans of Vice President Gore. The long-distance carriers responsible for funding this balked. They told the FCC that the universal service fund fees would henceforth appear as a line item on every one of their customers' bills.

The prospect of placing a highly visible new fee directly on consumer bills frightened the FCC. Consumers would likely complain, and those complaints would not be good for the FCC, or for the administration or Congress. The FCC forced the long-distance carriers to enter into closed-door negotiations. The public and the media were not invited.

The outcome of these negotiations was all too predictable: Long-distance carriers capitulated, gaining little more than a modest reduction in the size of the fund in 1997 and 1998 in return for an implicit promise to keep mention of the fees off consumer bills and to keep quiet about the entire matter.[5] The American consumer was the big loser, paying for a new, politically motivated program without even knowing it. Only after a few more years had elapsed, and the clear language of the statute requiring explicit funding was finally implemented, did an American consumer finally see a "universal service fee" show up on a monthly telephone bill. Not surprisingly, Congress subsequently viewed reforming the funding of universal service as a high priority.

Merger Reviews. Since the passage of the Act, the FCC has used the law as an instrument to insinuate itself into the merger review process. As will be discussed in detail in chapter 9, the FCC saw major communications industry mergers as an opportunity to impose conditions, often clearly unsupportable by statute, that were akin to company-specific rules applied in adjudicatory proceedings. These typically were promises from the merging parties to take actions that the FCC could not lawfully require by rule across the industry. Challenges by the parties to these conditions would likely have prevailed in court; however, none were forthcoming, since the parties had to "volunteer" the conditions in order to have their applications even considered.[6]

From 1997 to 2001, the FCC reviewed in detail the mergers of more than a dozen multibillion-dollar deals. The reviews involved substantial negotiations at the FCC, particularly on matters unrelated to the mergers, that went on behind closed doors, sometimes for weeks on end—invitation-only negotiations with a government that had little legal basis to engage in the negotiations in the first place. The normal procedures for the FCC to write new rules with public notice and comment under the Administrative Procedures Act were ignored; the public could not comment on proceedings it did not know about. Perhaps even more troubling, practically no one at the FCC thought that these negotiations were in the least bit a source of embarrassment.

The Exception That Proves the Rule. In the past few decades, the FCC has promulgated tens of thousands of orders and issued hundreds of thousands of letters, notices, and other written documents. Perhaps only one of these—changes in broadcast ownership rules in 2003—resulted in Congress taking swift action to reverse an FCC decision, and it did so largely in response to strong public involvement in the issue. The overruling of the FCC on deregulation of broadcast ownership was the exception that proved the rule that the agency normally escapes external discipline on behalf of the public.

Since the 1930s, the FCC has had complex arbitrary limits on broadcast license ownership unrelated to any specific demonstration of harm. These rules were gradually relaxed beginning in the 1970s and '80s. Had Al Gore been elected president in 2000, most industry observers expected the gradual relaxation to continue. With President Bush's election, the rules were widely expected to all but disappear under FCC Chairman Michael Powell.

Gannett, Scripps Howard, Tribune Company, NewsCorp, NBC, and many other companies rationally planned—and some even made—investments in anticipation of the changes, while those who wanted to keep the rules were resigned to defeat.

But on the road to deregulation, the FCC blinked. Rather than immediately adopt the changes widely anticipated in 2001, the agency sought more and more information on media ownership to add to what it had collected over decades. Rather than simply end them, the FCC considered how to replace one set of arbitrary ownership rules with another. Month after precious month was squandered.

In the midst of the FCC's equivocation, opponents of deregulation, led by Commissioner Michael Copps, launched a counterattack based on a grassroots movement of Americans fearful of media consolidation. The proceeding to change the broadcast ownership rules spanned several years and, unlike practically every other FCC proceeding, it evoked strong public reaction, much of it negative toward consolidation of media ownership. The proregulation forces spanned the political spectrum from community activists on the left to the National Rifle Association on the right. With each passing week, the prospects for continued regulation gained, as those for deregulation waned.

In June 2003, the FCC adopted Chairman Powell's proposed rules on a party-line vote. Within weeks, Congress overwhelmingly overrode part of the FCC's new rules addressing national ownership caps on television stations. The remaining changes were challenged in the Third Circuit Court of Appeals. That court held that the FCC had acted arbitrarily in adopting a "diversity index" and other puzzling rules. The Supreme Court refused to stay the decision of the circuit court, allowing even more irrational and arbitrary regulations from the 1970s to return.

In January 2001, no one could have described any scenario under which obsolete FCC broadcast ownership rules could remain in place years later. The crushing political defeat of even minor steps toward ownership deregulation emboldened the advocates of continued regulation and dispirited their opponents. The importance of the episode, which represented perhaps the only time that an FCC rule was overridden by Congress, is threefold. First, it demonstrated that if Congress were to hear from enough of the public, it could act to discipline the FCC. Second, it took the public being sufficiently engaged in an issue related to the FCC (which it rarely is) to capture Congress's attention. And third, it showed that the business community, which was divided on the broadcast ownership rules, is sometimes hesitant to complain openly to Congress about FCC decisions for fear of annoying the FCC. Business concerns did not drive the congressional decision in 2003.

Combined Powers Make Individuals Reluctant to Take Disputes to the FCC

In both the examples of the universal service fund and the merger review process, the FCC was able to stray outside the law both by exerting its combined powers and by hiding information from the public. In the universal service fund case, the agency used its substantial leverage in the closed-door negotiations into which it coerced the long-distance carriers. It threatened to retaliate in any number of areas through its powerful combination of legislative, administrative, and judicial powers if the carriers were to reveal the size of contributions on consumer bills.

An agency that only wrote rules, and did not enforce or adjudicate them, or that simply exercised the power of only one branch of government, would not have had such leverage over the carriers to compel their extralegal cooperation. An agency exercising the power of only one branch of government would likely have created a fund similar in size to the existing programs, and the fees to pay for it would have appeared explicitly on consumers' bills. It was precisely the threat to use the combined powers of government in a coordinated fashion that enabled the FCC to reach a specific outcome that one branch of government alone could not have lawfully imposed.

And in applying conditions to major mergers, the FCC injected arbitrary rulemaking authority into adjudicatory procedures.[7] In each case, the FCC leveraged its combined powers to compel parties into accepting a regulatory outcome that could not specifically be reached through a clear reading of the merger application before the commission.

The usual remedy of private parties for bad administrative decisions by the government is an appeal to court, and, indeed, appeals to court are available to individuals and firms dissatisfied with FCC decisions. As we shall see in more detail in chapter 7, the FCC often loses in court, an empirical observation that would seem to encourage more litigation, even on discretionary matters such as merger reviews. In at least one instance, a business trade association was bold enough to challenge an FCC merger decision, and the D.C. Circuit vacated the decision.[8]

The frequency of challenges to FCC decisions is far less than might be suggested by their success rate, though. At first blush, the failure of private parties to challenge the FCC in court seems counter to their own interests. On closer examination, however, it is clear that these parties are rationally exercising judgment, weighing the likelihood and value of ultimate success in complaining against the likelihood and cost of offending the government agency. Throughout the history of the FCC, regulated firms have rationally feared retribution.

For example, several firms initially challenged the patently unlawful aspects of the FCC's May 1997 universal service order in court. One by one, the plaintiffs dropped out of litigation, more afraid of retribution than concerned by direct costs. The remaining litigants narrowed the basis of the litigation until little remained of the original case. Even the Fifth Circuit's decision in *Texas Public Utility Counsel* seemed to have been made on the basis of matters outside the law.[9] To read the decision is to review page after page of detailed explanations of why the FCC rule is not a clear reading of the law. It sets the stage to remand the order, and then, in the end, perhaps in fear or exasperation, grants *Chevron* deference, the highest form of uncalibrated discretion available to a federal agency.

The absence of countervailing discipline to FCC actions from other branches of government and from the public has unfortunate consequences. The next three chapters examine those consequences.

7

Sloppy Rulemaking

The Telecommunications Act of 1996 assigned the FCC a seemingly impossible task: initiate multiple proceedings to write hundreds of pages of newly conceived rules, and conclude these proceedings with final rules in less than six months. It was a Herculean assignment, and the FCC accomplished it by the August 8, 1996, deadline.

But the initial applause for the timely completion soon gave way to consternation by many businesses and some in Congress as the details of the new rules were read. Expeditiously crafted as they were, they did not always clearly follow the letter of the Act. Hundreds of businesses, both new and incumbents, had been making investment decisions based on certain expectations of what the rules would be. When the rules were finally unveiled, some businesses cheered and expanded their operations. Others threatened litigation.

Expectations varied widely about whether the FCC would prevail in court in defending its new rules. Though not wild or untethered to any possible reading of the Act, they were sloppy, inexact interpretations of the statute, as would gradually be revealed as years passed. Despite public claims to the contrary, no one was certain how the courts would react.

Because its rulemaking power is combined with both enforcement and adjudication authority, the FCC had incentives in promulgating rules under the Telecommunications Act of 1996 that a purely rulemaking body would not have had. Unlike a purely rulemaking body, it could write rules vague enough to yield itself discretion in subsequent enforcement action or adjudication procedures under those same rules. The pattern of sloppy rules did not begin with the 1996 Act; it had long been in place under the Communications Act of 1934.

Of course, a government agency does not need such conflicting purposes to write sloppy rules. Insufficient resources or poor management often lead to that result. But where an agency has responsibilities that conflict with one another, additional resources or more robust management may not produce more precise and predictable rulemaking.

In this chapter, we examine the various aspects of the sloppy rulemaking that has resulted from the FCC's having combined powers of government:

- rules that have kept power at the agency for enforcement and adjudication;

- a history of written and unwritten rules;

- the "public interest" as the agency's authority;

- hidden taxes;

- a poor track record in court that has done little to improve the agency's rulemaking;

- consequential costs for both businesses and consumers; and

- no penalty for sloppy rules.

Rules That Kept Power at the FCC for Enforcement and Adjudication

In the years after the passage of the Telecommunications Act of 1996, disputes raged about whether the FCC's interpretation of it favored one industry group at the expense of another. Incumbent local exchange carriers claimed that competitive local exchange carriers were favored over them. The competitive local exchange carriers had the opposite view. The litigation of *AT&T v. Iowa Utilities Board* was animated with this form of industry dispute, of which there were many.

On one point, there was relatively little disagreement: The FCC rules consistently kept enforcement and adjudication responsibilities within the FCC rather than assigning them to other government bodies. The commission's entire structure of telephony regulation for local market-opening provisions, universal service, and permissions for the Bell Operating

Companies to offer long-distance services was structured for FCC administration and adjudication. Given that the FCC had the combined powers of
government, it is not surprising that it used its rulemaking authority to
extend the authority of its enforcement and adjudication activities.

There were occasional exceptions. For instance, the FCC granted states
substantial discretion over area code design and administration. But these rare
exceptions for state and local authority merely highlighted the extent to
which other governmental decisions were concentrated at the FCC. The D.C.
Circuit Court of Appeals would ultimately hold that the FCC did not even
have the authority to assign certain responsibilities under the Act to states.[1]

Moreover, the FCC not only wrote inexact rules in order to enhance its
administrative and adjudicatory responsibilities; it also used its administrative and adjudicatory responsibilities to enhance its rulemaking powers. In
an agency with purely administrative and enforcement responsibilities, it
would have been much easier to follow standardized procedures for administration and enforcement, but with additional responsibilities to attend to,
the FCC was tempted to look at any administrative or enforcement procedure as an opportunity to "improve" its written rules.

A History of Written and Unwritten Rules Facilitates Sloppiness

FCC rules, procedures, and practices operate both formally and informally.
The formal rules are the most visible. Formal FCC rules are recorded in the
Code of Federal Regulations; formal enforcement and adjudicatory orders
are recorded elsewhere, many publicly. In addition, the FCC issues formal
public notices and news releases.

Behind the formal rules are a great many unwritten, informal rules, often
addressing the details of how formal rules will be administered or enforced in
practice. Some of these are known to practitioners before the FCC, such as
the nuances of broadcast license applications or the procedures to contest a
specific large merger in the communications sector. Beginning in 1995, for
example, the FCC conducted several auctions each year. They were governed
by many rules, both formal and informal, and by letters issued by the FCC in
the context of specific circumstances related to each auction and its participants, along with informal guidance offered by FCC staff.

Other informal rules are not even widely known among practitioners but are known among political staff who understand the policy direction of the FCC. Thus, in 1998–99, the FCC informally decided that New York, despite applications from other states, would be the first to receive approval for a Bell Operating Company to offer interLATA (formally termed long-distance services).

The various forms of rules and interpretations are not inconsistent with one another; rather they reinforce one another, with the less formal rules and interpretations filling in gaps in the more formal ones. Their availability has enabled less precision, even sloppiness, in the writing of formal rules.

Informal FCC rules have three consistent characteristics: They are unwritten and thus have not been vetted through the normal Administrative Procedures Act process; they largely pertain to the administration, enforcement, or adjudication of formal FCC rules; and their importance and persistence are facilitated by the combination of the different branches of government by the FCC. If the different responsibilities of government were divided into different agencies, informal rules might still exist, but their importance and persistence would not be reinforced.

The "Public Interest" as Authority

Some of the sloppy rules written by the FCC are not derived from the Telecommunications Act of 1996 at all, and they have no specific authority other than the broad "public interest" obligations of the commission dating back to the Communications Act of 1934.[2]

In 2000, for example, the commission wrote a regulation requiring video program producers to include an aural description of visually presented information, such as the movement of actors in a scene, through a secondary audio programming (SAP) channel that could be heard only when that channel was activated using a device with SAP capability.[3] This was a well-intentioned idea, presumably for the benefit of visually impaired audiences, but the FCC simply had no legal authority to mandate it. The legal basis rested almost entirely on two polemical and vaguely worded sections of the Communications Act, 1 and 4(i).[4]

The Motion Picture Association of America and others challenged the FCC in court, and ultimately the D.C. Circuit Court of Appeals reversed the commission.[5] In his opinion, Chief Justice Edwards wisely quoted directly from Commissioner (later Chairman) Powell's dissent:

> It is important to emphasize that section 4(i) is not a stand-alone basis of authority and cannot be read in isolation. It is more akin to a "necessary and proper" clause. Section 4(i)'s authority must be "reasonably ancillary" to other express provisions. And, by its express terms, our exercise of that authority cannot be "inconsistent" with other provisions of the Act. The reason for these limitations is plain: Were an agency afforded carte blanche under such a broad provision, irrespective of subsequent congressional acts that did not squarely prohibit action, it would be able to expand greatly its regulatory reach.[6]

Unfortunately, video description is neither the first nor the last instance in which the FCC has relied almost exclusively on vague authority to engage in specific regulation not required by communications law and perhaps prohibited elsewhere.[7] Whenever the FCC expansively interprets the Communications Act of 1934 or the Telecommunications Act of 1996, it relies on the broad language in the Act to rationalize its chosen policy.

Hidden Taxes

In most democratic governments, the authority to impose taxes is limited to elected legislators. The ability of the electorate to remove officials who unfairly raise taxes is a fundamental concern of a democratic order. Legislators must balance the resistance of the electorate to taxes with the preferences of the same electorate for costly government services. Elected officials are uniquely positioned to weigh such considerations.

A government agency with a combination of government branch powers is able to develop its own sources of revenue to support its own programs. The FCC, of course, does not have elected officials, but it has substantial authority to write rules requiring fees that are, for all intents and purposes, taxes.

In the late 1990s, Ray Sadie was an independent radio broadcaster in Louisiana.[8] He frequently complained to the FCC about his radio license fees going up every year, even though he did not get any additional service from the FCC in exchange for the increases.

Sadie had a legitimate complaint. A government fee is supposed to pay the cost of providing a specific service narrowly benefiting the class paying the fee. Thus, driver's license fees are supposed to cover some of the costs of a motor vehicle agency's issuance of driver's licenses. It is usually not intended to pay for the state's general revenue, or even the costs of building and maintaining the roads that the driver will use. A state might collect additional revenue from issuing driver's licenses above the cost of providing licenses but, in legal parlance, those excess receipts would constitute a *tax*, not a fee, because they would have been raised to serve the state generally, not just the people issued driver's licenses.

At the FCC, licensing, while a major activity, consumes much less than half of the commission's resources. Far more resources are absorbed by rule-making, enforcement, research, litigation, and other activities, which typically do not generate receipts and which, until roughly a decade ago, were largely funded from general revenues appropriated by Congress. In recent years, however, Congress has found that funding more of the FCC's activities with license and other fees improves Congress's own score in terms of fiscal responsibility. The FCC's abuse of powers in charging fees that are really taxes happens to serve the political purposes of Congress.

Because it enjoys the powers of all three branches of government, the FCC has the means to fund operations that affect the entire country by charging a relatively small number of individuals who happen to hold FCC licenses. This means that Ray Sadie, and thousands of other people like him, pay not only for the administrative cost to service the licenses from which they receive a benefit, but for the cost of an entire agency from which they receive no benefit. They have good reason to be upset about bearing costs amounting to more than $200 million a year, each dollar of which goes to the government for a service that costs the government less than a dime.[9] A purely rulemaking body would not be in a position to relabel taxes as user fees this way. It would have to obtain its own funds from

Congress, rather than look to separate enforcement or adjudication entities for contributions.

As we have already seen in chapter 5, an even bigger tax that the FCC pretends is a fee funds the schools and libraries universal service program. While most federal programs for schools and libraries are appropriately funded out of general revenues, this program, which costs over $2 billion annually, is funded by "fees" from telephone consumers. In turn, the money is spent not to provide services to telephone consumers, but to build infrastructure for schools and libraries. There is no rational boundary to the size or scope of the program, whose boundaries are set by the commission. If the FCC has the authority to impose more than $2 billion worth of fees on telephone consumers for the universal service program, why not $20 billion?

A Poor Track Record in Court Has Done Little to Improve Rulemaking

As we have seen, parties before the FCC are strongly discouraged from challenging the agency because its combination of legislative, executive, and judicial powers gives it ample opportunities to deflect court challenges. Yet some do mount challenges under the Act, because of the frailty of the commission's legal reasoning in promulgating rules and its poor record in court.

By all accounts, the FCC has never had the best track record in court, and its success rate in major cases does not seem to have improved with its implementation of the Act. FCC decisions related to telephone companies, such as unbundled network elements under sections 251 and 252, reciprocal compensation, a defensible approach to customer proprietary network information (CPNI), and media ownership limits are areas in which the agency has failed court review more than once. Regardless of whether the cause of the court defeats has been statutory interpretive errors on the part of the commission or even of the courts reviewing the appeals, the FCC has been slow to rewrite its rules to come into compliance with court decisions.

Measuring the litigation success rate of a government agency in court is not a simple exercise. Some cases are more important and central to an agency's operations than others. In February 2002, for instance, the FCC won *Grid Radio v. FCC* and lost *Fox Television Stations v. FCC*.[10] While it may appear that the FCC was batting .500 that month, *Grid Radio* was a finding of relatively little consequence that the FCC could lawfully block the broadcasts of an unlicensed pirate radio station, while *Fox Television Stations* remanded to the commission important broadcast ownership rules.

Moreover, a government agency may go through multiple episodes of litigation and receive multiple court opinions regarding the same or related issues, with not every opinion an unambiguous victory or loss. When a court issues a remand to the FCC, it is more often a remand of only part of an FCC order rather than the entire order.[11] With a partial remand, all sides can and do claim victory.[12] Even a partial remand, however, places a burden on the FCC to respond to the court.

Until the legal issues are resolved, either a remand or court reversal exacerbates legal uncertainty at the FCC in at least three ways. First, a defeat in court, including even a partial remand, demonstrates that practically any part of an FCC decision is subject to review and revision, and thus may not be considered permanent. Second, for the specific portion of an FCC order that is remanded or reversed, outside parties have little guidance as to the likely outcome. Third, to the extent the FCC is slow to respond, as it often is, the agency prolongs a costly period of uncertainty.

For all of these reasons, it is not surprising that an accurate statistical representation of the FCC's litigation success rate is difficult to find. Tables 7.1 and 7.2 provide an estimate drawn from court opinions from 1997 through 2002, published on the FCC's Web site, in which the agency was a principal party. This sample appears to include all Supreme Court and circuit court opinions, and some, but not all, lower court opinions.[13] Each opinion is placed in one of two categories: an "unqualified victory," where an FCC position was completely upheld; or "other," where the court reversed or remanded at least part of an FCC decision. Further, the opinions are divided between matters directly related to the 1996 Act and those that were not.

Table 7.1 indicates that the FCC is approximately twice as likely to suffer a setback on litigation related to the 1996 Act as on that related to other matters. Moreover, most of the reversals suffered by the FCC unrelated to the 1996 Act pertain to the specific circumstances of individual licensees, not to general rulemakings that affect an entire industry. In contrast, most of the reversals related to the Act pertain to the FCC's broad rulemakings and the interpretations of large portions of the Act.

TABLE 7.1

COURT VICTORIES OF THE FCC IN WHICH THE FCC OR
THE UNITED STATES IS A NAMED PARTY

	Related to 1996 Act		Unrelated to 1996 Act		Total	
	Unqualified victory	Other	Unqualified victory	Other	Unqualified victory	Other
1997	1	7	22	8	23	15
1998	5	2	19	5	24	7
1999	5	5	17	5	22	10
2000	7	7	23	6	30	13
2001	6	7	15	6	21	13
2002 (through October 1)	5	9	7	1	12	10
Total	29	37	103	31	132	68

SOURCE: Based on author's calculations from review of cases listed in FCC, Office of General Counsel, "FCC & FRC Reported Cases, 1928–2002," December 12, 2003, http://www.fcc.gov/ogc/caselist.html (accessed October 13, 2005). The FCC list omits many bankruptcy court and district court opinions. "Unqualified" victory means that no part of the court decision reversed or remanded any part of any FCC decision.

New laws are tempered through interpretation and court review. Until then, they remain brittle. It is not entirely surprising that a government agency would suffer some legal reversals during implementation of a new law such as the Act. What is surprising, however, is just how long it is taking the FCC to transform the Act from "unsettled" to "settled" law. While 1997 was clearly the weakest year for the FCC's interpretation of the Act, the pattern of losses has not measurably improved since then. In addition, the summary in table 7.1 does not reveal the length of time it takes the FCC to correct its mistakes in implementation. Important issues remain unresolved years after courts have found FCC rules inconsistent with the Act.

It would be reasonable to expect new legislation to lead to a burst of litigation until all aspects of the law have been settled. By itself, table 7.1 suggests the opposite: there has not been such an explosion. An average of little more than ten opinions a year hardly seems a major increase in court activity. However, this may only be evidence that potential litigants are avoiding

TABLE 7.2

CATEGORIES OF CASES RELATED TO THE TELECOMMUNICATIONS ACT OF
1996 IN WHICH THE FCC OR THE UNITED STATES IS A NAMED PARTY

	Constitutionality of Statute		FCC in Exercise of Legislative Authority		FCC in Exercise of Adjudicatory Authority		FCC in Exercise of Combined Authority	
	Unquali-fied FCC victory	Other	Unquali-fied FCC victory	Other	Unquali-fied FCC victory	Other	Unquali-fied FCC victory	Other
1997		2	1	4		1		
1998	1		2	2			2	
1999			2	5	1		2	
2000		1	4	5	1	1	2	
2001			3	4	3	2		1
2002 (through October)			3	7	2	1		1
Total	**1**	**3**	**15**	**27**	**7**	**5**	**6**	**2**

SOURCE: Based on author's calculations from review of cases listed in FCC, Office of General Counsel, "FCC & FRC Reported Cases, 1928–2002," December 12, 2003, http://www.fcc.gov/ogc/caselist.html (accessed October 13, 2005). The FCC list omits many bankruptcy court and district court opinions. "Unqualified" victory means that no part of the court decision reversed or remanded any part of any FCC decision.

direct confrontations with the FCC. Table 7.1 does not reveal the large increase in litigation related to the Act in which the FCC is not a named party. Much of this litigation is between private parties and state regulators, supposedly about state implementation of the Act, or between private parties themselves, disputing the Act's provisions.[14] Private parties may be seeking the results they wish to obtain from court action against the FCC through litigation against parties other than the FCC so as to yield a legal remedy without antagonizing a feared regulatory agency.

Table 7.1 also masks differences in the types of cases in which the FCC is likely to be affirmed and those in which it is more likely to be reversed. Table 7.2 addresses this by dividing the sixty-four cases related to the Telecommunications Act of 1996 into different types. Four cases are related to the constitutionality of the statutory language, for which the FCC has no responsibility. Forty are related to judicial reviews of FCC rulemakings. Eleven opinions relate to FCC decisions interpreting existing commission rules, and eight pertain to FCC decisions that combine aspects of the legislative, executive, and judicial authority of the commission.

Table 7.2 reveals a clear difference in the FCC's success rate on challenges related to its rulemaking capacity and everything else. In its rulemaking capacity, the FCC has little better than a one-in-three chance of being completely supported by court opinion, while in other matters, it is more likely than not to be successful in court. Moreover, many of its losses in matters unrelated to the Act pertain to the constitutionality or legality of FCC rules.

Much of this has been unnecessary. If the FCC would base its decisions on the simplest and most literal interpretation of statutes rather than aiming for specific policy outcomes, its odds in court would likely improve substantially. Moreover, the commission could seek opinions from a court in *advance* of final implementation of its rules to gain additional assurance of their validity. But the FCC has not done that. Despite ample evidence of the inadequacy of its rulemaking, the commission has had little incentive to improve its efforts. Even though practically all of the many decisions the FCC has made under the Act could have been challenged as falling outside the law, it has remained relatively unmolested by the courts.

Why is that? For most businesses, the risks of taking the FCC to court have been prohibitive. The costs of private litigation against taxpayer-sponsored litigation are high, and the course of litigation for each decision could easily take years and have an unknown outcome. Furthermore, the agency has held enormous influence over the fate of firms, both through litigation and its ability to write or enforce rules more favorable to one firm than another. Even many parties that initially prevailed against the commission in court for its interpretation of provisions of the Act have failed to capitalize on their legal victories, because the FCC's power ultimately to rewrite rules and enforce them as it chooses has often rendered the victories Pyrrhic.

With such high stakes, many businesses have preferred and sought the comfort of a negotiated settlement with the FCC, finding it better to have the certainty of some revenue even if the courts seemed willing to entertain the prospect of awarding them substantially more money. The FCC, for its part, could view with some satisfaction the fact that despite repeated losses in court, it could still negotiate a final settlement with parties on the implementation of the Act, a settlement often not clearly within the law any more than the rule originally in question was. With such an outcome, what incentive did the commission have to write better rules?

Consequential Costs for Both Businesses and Consumers

The sloppiness of the rulemaking at the FCC affects other laws as well. In the mid-1990s, the House Committee on Commerce conducted a survey of most of the federal agencies under its jurisdiction. The survey found that none of the agencies had procedures in place to evaluate prospectively the benefits and costs of either new or existing regulations.[15] Indeed, no agency, including the FCC, could point to a single regulation for which there was even an effort at a complete written accounting of costs and benefits associated with such regulations.

Of course, it is impossible to quantify many, much less all, of the potential costs and benefits of a federal regulation. Without at least a rough description of the expected outcome, it is impossible to know whether a rule is even expected to have more benefits than costs from the outset. No one, not government or businesses or private individuals, has any basis for knowing whether these rules meet even a minimum standard of economic rationality; nor is it possible for anyone to determine whether, years later, a rule is delivering its intended effect.

Some federal laws have attempted to remedy this problem. For example, the Small Business Regulatory Enforcement Fairness Act (SBREFA) requires agencies to evaluate the effect of new regulations on small businesses. Even the FCC includes an SBREFA analysis with each new regulation, but these evaluations are reported in boilerplate forms, enlightening neither the reader nor the staffer who filled out the form. The Small Business Administration has complained to the FCC about its implementation of SBREFA, to no avail.

The FCC's sloppy rulemaking has had a deleterious effect on business and business venture that has been quite costly, too. Under the Act, competition properly placed in the market was relocated to the courtroom as rule after rule was called into question. With the arrival of hundreds of entrants to the telecommunications industry after the Act was passed, new and incumbent carriers quickly found that their property and contract rights were often ambiguous. None knew their legal rights a day in advance, much less the time required to accommodate business planning cycles. During pending litigation, companies could take extreme postures as a tactical move against vulnerable rivals, sometimes refusing to make payments on obligations in dispute. The net result was that smaller firms whose business plans relied largely on issues in litigation were soon out of business. The uncertainty arising from erroneous implementation of the law served to spook the investment community as well.

The FCC itself has suffered no penalty or cost for failing to follow statutory language precisely. In 1998, for example, the commission failed to conduct a review of all telecommunications regulations, as required by section 11 of the Act, because its chairman decided that personnel were better used on other assignments.[16] The biennial review was carried out only on a limited basis in 2000.[17] The costs of complying with the regulatory review section of the Act were perceived as too great given the other responsibilities of the agency, many of which were not rulemaking in nature. For the commission, there was no penalty for noncompliance, and so the law became little more than a menu from which the agency might order implementation as it desired, rendering Congress's efforts to write effective legislation a hollow exercise.

To parties outside the FCC, there may well have been substantial costs to the agency's noncompliance, but these were never considered in the decision to skip the section 11 requirement. They ended up being paid by companies that had waited for the results of regulatory review before deciding on which rules to challenge.

Another instance of noncompliance by the FCC with a statutory deadline involved the auction of spectrum. The fiscal year 2000 Consolidated Appropriations Law instructed the FCC to hold an auction for spectrum licenses in the 700 MHz range so that funds would be received by the Treasury Department before September 30, 2000.[18] The language in the statute was unambiguous, yet in a series of commission orders, the FCC postponed the auction, claiming that waiting would substantially increase the government's auction revenue receipts. The statutory language, however, did not give the FCC the discretion to decide whether to obey the law or not, no matter how meritorious its judgment might have been.

Moreover, in this case, the FCC's judgment to disobey the law was almost certainly economically disastrous. The delay led to a loss, not a gain, in government receipts. Further, the failure to auction the 700 Mhz spectrum led to a protracted political battle in Congress over the transition from analog to digital television, with the 700 Mhz spectrum held hostage. More than five years later, rights to the spectrum have yet to be auctioned. Had the rights to the spectrum been auctioned in 2000, the transition to digital television would be much further along than it is today.

The FCC's alleged concern with maximizing revenues by postponing the auction stemmed from its administrative and enforcement responsibilities in conducting the auctions and overseeing the collection of receipts. If the body writing the rules for conducting the auctions were not also the body collecting the receipts, the rulemaking body might have been more inclined to follow the law.

The rationale that the FCC used to break the law in each of these instances was a balancing-of-interests argument.[19] It simply did so, on its own initiative, without public notice or comment, and ended up costing businesses and the public a great deal.

Combination of Powers and Sloppy Rules

The combination of powers at the FCC did not alone bring about inexact, sloppy rules, but it created an environment at the agency in which they could be written and reinforced through administration and adjudication carried out under them. As we have already seen, the inexact rules in turn led to many great uncertainties: uncertainty about which rules applied under various situations in communications markets; uncertainty about how courts would interpret them; and uncertainty in the minds of investors about the stability of investments in the communications sector. In the following chapter, these uncertainties and their connection with the combination of powers at the FCC will be further explored.

8

Unpredictable FCC Rules and
Communications Law

Between 1996 and 2000, investors directed countless billions of dollars to the communications sector. Much of the investment went to well-known, publicly traded communications companies, such as AT&T, Sprint, BellSouth, and NewsCorp. Much went to well-known corporations that dabbled in communications, such as Enron. Some went to lesser-known companies, many privately held, and some went to companies that never evolved beyond a business plan.

All of these investments went to businesses with plans credible enough to attract them. Within a few years, however, many proved to have poor returns; some even became worthless. Many factors contributed to the downturn in communications sector investments between 2000 and 2002. Bad business plans, poor management, poor execution, and unscrupulous accounting doubtlessly accounted for some bad investments. But for each of the many plausible explanations, poor performance in any one area should have been offset by rich returns for businesses that performed well in that area. This did not generally happen. While a few companies in the communications sector weathered the downturn from 2000 to 2002 well, most did not.

All of these businesses had at least one common characteristic: They were exposed to unpredictable FCC rules and communications law. This uncertainty contributed to the problems of the communications companies during this period, and the combination of powers at the FCC contributed to the uncertainty.

Below, we examine a few particular examples that illustrate the legal uncertainty generated by the FCC, including:

- uncertainty and delays from sloppy rules;

- uncertainty of enforcement;

- uncertainty of adjudication;

- loss of valuable time; and

- the costs of negotiations and settlements as a result of uncertainty.

Uncertainty and Delays from Sloppy Rules

One of the purposes of the 1996 Act was to establish clear rules in many areas where there were no rules. Despite the best of intentions, the results were exactly the opposite. Practically everywhere that the FCC established rules, the net result was more rather than less uncertainty, as private parties endlessly litigated decisions in court. As we have seen, because the FCC was less careful than it should have been in promulgating these rules, it never had—nor did anyone in business have—complete confidence that it would prevail in court.

The uncertainty of FCC rules was reinforced by the combination of powers; a separate rulemaking body might have been more exact in writing rules, and thus created less uncertainty about their legal status. The result was devastating to many business plans. Few aspects of the implementation of the 1996 Act undermined confidence in communications markets more than the uncertainty surrounding the legal rights and responsibilities of communications companies.

One example of this phenomenon is the section 271 process, which will be discussed in greater detail in chapter 9. Before passage of the Telecommunications Act of 1996, the Bell Operating Companies (NYNEX, BellAtlantic, BellSouth, Ameritech, SBC, U.S.West, and Pacific Bell in 1996) could not offer long-distance (formally termed interLATA) services. The Act allowed them to apply to the FCC for the opportunity to offer these services—a valuable opportunity without which they would be handicapped relative to new entrants who could immediately offer such services. During the period 1996–2002, the long-distance entry of Bell Operating Companies was one of the major issues before the FCC.

The Act spells out in detail the requirements for long-distance entry of Bell Operating Companies in section 271 on a state-by-state basis. It even admonishes the FCC not to embellish or omit them; yet in a series of section 271 decisions, the FCC both added to and subtracted from these requirements.[1] The malleability of FCC standards created uncertainty both for the Bell Operating Companies and for challengers to BOC applications. Because the FCC was both the reviewing agency and the agency writing the rules to implement section 271, the plasticity of its interpretation of the law gave the agency too much discretion.

Had the responsibility for writing rules under the Act been separated from the responsibility for enforcing them and adjudicating individual issues under them, there is every reason to believe that those rules would have been clearer and more legally defensible, and would have delivered more predictable outcomes for regulated entities.

Such FCC-created uncertainty imposes substantial costs on telecommunications markets, investors in those markets, and the consumers they serve. Table 8.1 presents a few of the issues central to legal rights within the telecommunications sector that have remained under a cloud for years. The first column in the table lists issues of interest to many telecommunications carriers. The second column contains the date of the initial FCC order, if any, addressing each issue. The third contains the date of the first clear judicial setback on the issue, and the fourth gives the date the FCC reconciled all of the competing interests with respect to the issue in an order that would withstand court scrutiny.

Table 8.1 indicates two periods of uncertainty for companies making investments during 1996–2002. The first began with the initial issuance of an FCC rule and ended when the FCC rule suffered a significant setback in court. During much, if not all, of this period, businesses understood both that the FCC had a rule in mind and that that rule was being challenged in court. They probably did not have a clear sense of the likelihood of an FCC victory on the issue in court since, as we have seen, the FCC loses about half of its cases.

Many businesses developed plans based on the initial rules set forth in table 8.1. In practically every instance, the initial FCC rule or order did not fail court review for many months or even years—substantial time periods during which many businesses might have reasonably developed plans

TABLE 8.1

SELECTED ISSUES UNDER THE ACT WITH IMPLICIT PROPERTY
AND CONTRACT RIGHTS SUBJECT TO PROLONGED PERIODS OF
UNCERTAINTY UNDER FCC AND COURT DECISIONS

Issue	Date of initial FCC rule	Date of initial court uncertainty	Resolution of uncertainty as of Nov. 1, 2002	Comments
Reciprocal compensation	August 8, 1996[2]	March 24, 2000[3]	Unresolved	Intermediate FCC decisions.[4] Intermediate court decisions.[5]
Unbundled Network Element list	August 8, 1996[6]	Jan. 25, 1996[6]	Unresolved 1999[7]	FCC won initial victories on UNE list at the 8th Circuit,[8] but lost subsequent cases.[9]
Collocation	August 8, 1996[10]	March 17, 2000[11]	June 18, 2002[12]	
Line-sharing requirements	Nov. 18, 1999[13]	May 24, 2002[14]	Unresolved	
Unbundled Network Element pricing	August 8, 1996[15]	July 18, 1997[16]	May 13, 2002[17]	Intermediate court decisions.[18]
Customer Proprietary Network Information	Feb. 19, 1998[19]	August 18, 1999[20]	July 25, 2002[21]	
Validity of price-squeeze argument in objections to section 271 applications	Jan. 22, 2001[22]	Dec. 28, 2001[23]	Unresolved	Intermediate court decisions.[24]
Pay phone compensation arrangements	Sept. 20, 1996[25]	July 1, 1997[26]	Unresolved	Intermediate court decisions.[27]

SOURCE: Author's research.

predicated upon continuation of those particular rules. During this first period of uncertainty (represented by the time period between the third column and the second column), investments could be made with the expectation of a static rule environment because the FCC had yet to be proved incapable of writing a rule that could withstand court review. Moreover, the burden of proof to find a rule deficient fell on the challenging party. Furthermore, the FCC received *Chevron* deference on its rule-making authority. Thus, there was much reason to believe that the FCC rule would be upheld, and investment decisions assuming so were plausibly rational.

The second period of uncertainty began with the initial court setback for the FCC and continued until a final resolution was determined. As can be seen in table 8.1, few of these issues found resolution by the end of 2002. Whenever a court review found part or all of an FCC rule to be deficient, the FCC failed to construct a resolution satisfactory to the court in a timely manner. Either appeals or remand actions, or both, would last for years. The burden of proof during this second period largely shifted back to the FCC, which then had to develop rules able to withstand court scrutiny.

Plans made by businesses during this second period that involved more than one of the issues listed in table 8.1 were forced to rely on what were little better than hunches about future regulatory regimes—hardly a basis for optimal investment decision-making. As FCC court defeats mounted in the years following the Act, the inventory of unresolved issues grew. The larger the inventory of unresolved issues, the more tangled the web of uncertainty facing investors, and the more difficulty and cost any investor in the communications sector faced in finding capital. Resolving one or even two or three of the issues in table 8.1 did not necessarily remove all of the regulatory uncertainty facing many firms in the industry. Table 8.1 lists only selected items among a much larger set of issues under dispute at the FCC. Moreover, as the second period of uncertainty extended for years, some investors eventually became skeptical that the FCC would ever be capable of providing conditions of regulatory certainty.

In recent years, most of the issues in table 8.1 have eventually been resolved or are actively being addressed, albeit slowly. Resolution of those still open, however, may never be final. As the law evolves, new court challenges may yet surface; areas of law that appear to be settled today may go back into a state of suspended animation. Even more likely, the FCC may, through its procedures, continue to change its own rules, and with each change expose the rules to fresh challenges.

The slow response to court defeats is almost certainly related to the structure of the FCC. Most defeats related to the Act pertain to its rule-making activities. (See table 8.2.) An agency that has no authority except to write rules would be more likely to remedy losses in court quickly than an agency such as the FCC, which has multiple and separate agendas of enforcement and adjudication based on existing and contemplated rules serving its various purposes. Indeed, informal rules and enforcement at the FCC ultimately must fill the gap from the inexact rulemakings.

Table 8.1 is by no means a comprehensive list of the uncertainties facing telecommunications carriers, nor is it a comprehensive list of issues that the FCC is actively reviewing. Many other issues—treatment of high-speed data services (broadband), wireless technologies, universal service—are all under FCC review at any given time. Collectively, these unresolved issues generate a cloud of uncertainty that hangs over all investments in the telecommunications sector. This may not be the primary cause of decreased industry valuations since passage of the Act, but it cannot be entirely coincidental either. Imagine being presented a choice of two investment opportunities. An FCC rule lies in the critical path of one but not the other. What premium would an investor demand for the FCC-impaired investment?

The pattern of uncertainty related to rulemaking is found in media regulation as well. Table 8.2 is similar to table 8.1, with the same set of five columns, except that it pertains to the broadcast and cable industries. Once again, the FCC has been remarkably slow to reconcile the issues following a defeat in court.

As of 2005, the FCC, despite repeated court defeats, has yet to promulgate regulations to implement many of the issues in tables 8.1 and 8.2. Hundreds of firms rationally developed business plans around initial FCC rules, only to remain uncertain years later which rules will actually be in place. As businesses have painfully discovered, FCC rules related to the Act can be overturned by courts or at the collective whim of a new or even the same set of commissioners.

TABLE 8.2

SELECTED ISSUES RELATED TO BROADCASTING OR CABLE
OPERATIONS UNDER THE ACT WITH IMPLICIT PROPERTY AND
CONTRACT RIGHTS SUBJECT TO PROLONGED PERIODS OF
UNCERTAINTY UNDER FCC AND COURT DECISIONS
(THROUGH OCTOBER 2002)

Issue	Date of initial FCC rule	Date of initial court uncertainty	Resolution of uncertainty as of Nov. 1, 2002	Comments
Cable MSO ownership limits	1992[28] FCC rule, 1993[29]	1993[30]	Unresolved	Rules subject to review by FCC biannually under section 202(h); never fully reviewed. Intermediate FCC decisions.[31] Intermediate court decisions.[32]
National broadcast television ownership limits	1940s	June 21, 2002[33]	Unresolved	Rules subject to review by FCC biannually under section 202(h). Intermediate decisions.[34]
Newspaper cross-ownership limits	1970s	1990s	Unresolved	Rules subject to review by FCC biannually under section 202(h); never fully reviewed.
Pole attachments		April 11, 2000[35]	Unresolved intermediate decisions [36]	

SOURCE: Author's research.

Uncertainty of Enforcement

Rulemakings are not the only source of uncertainty at the FCC. Enforcement is another. The FCC has some rules that are predictably enforced, such as those pertaining to power limits on broadcast transmission or safety lighting on broadcast towers. Others, such as broadcast indecency rules, are intermittently enforced. Still others are rarely enforced, such as record-keeping requirements for continuing property records for telecommunications carriers (see chapter 9). As a result, regulated entities are often uncertain about which FCC rules will be enforced and which will not. Legal practitioners before the commission often rely on informal guidance from its staff about enforcement of rules.

The discretionary enforcement of rules by the FCC reinforces its combined powers of government. A purely enforcement agency would have little incentive to choose enforcement policies that reinforced its rulemaking objectives or that lightened its adjudicatory responsibilities. The FCC, however, has such incentives.

Uncertainty of Adjudication

Private parties often complain about the alleged failure of regulated entities to comply with all aspects of a regulation. For example, many telephone companies informally complain that other telephone companies are not complying with aspects of commission rules, or a broadcast network affiliate may informally complain that a network is abusing FCC rules on the role of broadcast networks. The FCC has many volumes of regulations that some private parties believe are not always followed.

Yet informal dissatisfaction with rule compliance only infrequently translates into formal complaints at the FCC. Administrative costs account to some extent for this paucity. It is costly for a firm to file a formal complaint, and its resolution could take months or even years. Mostly, however, private parties are reluctant to file formal complaints with the FCC because many are discouraged from doing so by the agency itself. Formal complaints take substantial FCC staff resources to resolve promptly. With its combined powers of government, the agency can choose to invest relatively few resources in this manner, as compared to one whose only responsibility is to resolve disputes. As a result, regulated businesses face not only uncertain rules that are inexactly written, but also uncertain adjudication of disputes under those rules.

In addition, although several sections of the Communications Act of 1934 provide for the filing and resolution of complaints, they are largely dysfunctional.[37] Similar complaint processes exist in state regulatory agencies. Lack of effect has led to disuse, and even many seasoned communications lawyers seem unaware of the full range of the FCC's, or a state regulatory agency's, complaint processes. Those who are familiar with these procedures flatly state that they do not work, and that their clients would be out of business long before a complaint would ever be resolved. Private parties resort instead to private negotiations with the allegedly offending parties, or turn their disputes over to other government bodies.

As a result, the FCC commissioners are often left to hear new complaints regarding old problems for which there is no written record in the bureaus. During proceedings to review an application of a Bell Operating Company for permission to offer long-distance services, for example,[38] the FCC was flooded with informal complaints of bad and unlawful behavior, but few of these had ever initially been formally lodged, either with a state regulatory agency or with the FCC Common Carrier Bureau.[39]

Loss of Valuable Time

Regulated businesses large and small have something in common: They have lost millions of dollars as a result of delayed decision-making by the FCC. Businesses petition for licenses, license transfers, and many other matters because they have business plans that depend on specific FCC actions. Even in a case where the commission has ultimately reached a favorable decision, its delay in reaching it may have substantially eroded the return on an investment that was dependent upon the timely institution of that decision. Some delays hamper a business's ability to sell its products or services, reducing its revenue streams. Most business plans cannot be switched on the moment an FCC approval is obtained. Costs of personnel, plant, and equipment accrue during the wait. All too often, a business discovers that the FCC has not fully granted its petition, and plans are dashed or further delayed pending a costly and time-consuming court appeals process.

While these delays may be lawful, they are by no means necessary. The Communications Act specifically encourages the FCC to make decisions within ninety days, but this rarely happens.[40]

TABLE 8.3

DELAYS ASSOCIATED WITH MERGERS REVIEWED BY THE FCC
LICENSE TRANSFER APPLICATIONS
1997–2002

	Number of mergers	Average delay in days	Median delay in days
Commission-level decisions	25	296.0	248.0
Delegated decisions	23	144.7	126.5
All decisions	48	223.6	188.5

SOURCE: See appendix.

The delays are particularly noticeable in the case of license transfers, most of which are ultimately granted. The FCC has issued hundreds of thousands of licenses. Each time a license shifts from one holder to another, a formal transfer must occur.[41] Each year, more than ten thousand licenses are transferred, mostly on a routine basis in a matter of few months, including a public notice and comment period.

The FCC takes a few of these transfers, however—particularly those involving major mergers—and subjects them to special and arbitrary review. The appendix lists by industry sector some of the major mergers reviewed by the FCC. The length of these delays ranges from 73 to 730 days. Of the forty-eight mergers listed, only five took 90 days or less to review, as directed by the Act.

As shown in table 8.3, the delays in 1997–2002 averaged nearly 224 days, and the median delay was nearly 190 days. Thus, more than half lasted more than half a year—twice as long as the Communications Act permits. There was no clear industry sector pattern; a merger in any sector could take substantial time, although those license transfers handled on delegated authority tended to take substantially less time than those reviewed by the full commission. The median delay for license transfers decided by the full commission was 248 days, while that of those on delegated authority was only half that long. Thus, a license transfer handled on delegated authority tended to be only one month too long, while those decided by the full commission were typically four months too long.

Exacerbating the delays further is the unpredictability of dispute adjudications and their frequent entanglement with either rulemaking or enforcement proceedings. The FCC uses its merger review process to reinforce its rulemaking, enforcement, and adjudication activities by sometimes placing conditions on mergers. As seen in the appendix, simple license transfers between private parties, usually treated by the FCC as adjudications, often result in conditions unrelated to the transfer.

The Costs of Negotiations and Settlements as a Result of Uncertainty

Where rules are inexact and uncertain, private parties under those rules may negotiate outcomes with the FCC simply to gain some certainty. Some of these obligations, which are not required by law, are negotiated by a private party with the FCC as a way to get the agency to move on an item that the commission is legally bound to complete anyway.

Thus, practically every major merger "reviewed" by the FCC entails substantial concessions made by applicant parties.[42] They range from limiting future business operations to selling assets to individuals selected by the commission. Without the FCC, these mergers would still have been reviewed by federal and state antitrust authorities that probably would have forced concessions as well. Those antitrust concessions would have been made in accordance with antitrust case law, however, and would have had some economic rationale.

The additional concessions that are made above and beyond antitrust requirements to accommodate the FCC do not abide anything other than the FCC policy agenda, and thus have a political rather than an economic rationale. Furthermore, this political rationale may in fact be economically irrational. No precise measure can be made of the costs of these extra concessions, but in some transactions—WorldCom-MCI, AT&T MediaOne, SBC-Ameritech, Bell Atlantic–GTE, AOL–Time Warner—they were certainly worth billions of dollars. Some concessions are formalized in commission orders. Others are unwritten. Arranged to be implemented after approval, they are enforceable only as long as anyone at the commission remembers them.

The combined powers of the FCC led to great uncertainty about how rules, enforcement, and adjudications would be handled. The uncertainty was not blind and random. As we will see in the following chapter, the combination of powers gave the FCC at least the appearance of preferential or discriminatory treatment of regulated businesses.

9

An Appearance of Discriminatory Treatment by the FCC

Individuals or businesses appearing before a government agency are sensitive to how they are treated in governmental processes. We want to be treated no worse than others. If we have evidence that a government agency is discriminating against us individually, most of us will complain, either directly to that agency or to other agencies of government.

Even government discretion is often limited by specific rules, and discretionary activities may require approval of another branch of government. Thus, a public library cannot use its discretion to charge overdue fines in excess of rates as posted. The police department cannot use its own discretion to search private property without a court-approved search warrant. Nor can an antitrust agency use its discretion to block a merger of two companies without a trial in federal court.

In a government with separated powers, each branch will monitor the behavior of government agencies for acts of favoritism and discrimination in the application of laws. The mere presence of such monitoring tends to discourage an agency from engaging in discriminatory behavior.

Individuals and businesses have few venues to complain of unequal treatment in appearing before an agency such as the FCC that combines all of the powers of government. As we have seen in previous chapters, the other branches of government are unlikely to discipline the FCC.

The FCC does not actively seek to use its discretion to engage in discriminatory activities, nor is it consciously used as a tool for improper purposes. But left unchecked and beyond review, discretion at the FCC and other government agencies has unfortunate consequences. These are most easily seen with:

- discriminatory enforcement, and

- discriminatory adjudicatory proceedings.

Discriminatory Enforcement

Discrimination in the administration and enforcement of laws is not formally sanctioned. It exists only informally, where necessary discretion in the administration of government transforms into unnecessary disparate treatment of similarly situated individuals and businesses.

The Fourteenth Amendment prohibits most forms of overt discrimination; however, Congress occasionally defines certain classes of businesses or individuals as eligible for or subject to special legal treatment, with predictable benefits or harms. Legal precedent guides Congress and other legislative bodies as to which types and for what purposes creation of such legal classes is permitted. This selectivity always bears a high burden of proof when confronted with court review.

Given Congress's inability to escape court review for compliance with the Fourteenth Amendment, it comes as no surprise that the Telecommunications Act of 1996 does not require or even suggest that the FCC write rules discriminating between or among individual regulated entities. Other than the Bell Operating Companies, the Act does not establish classes that are defined by a specific list of companies.[1]

The FCC does occasionally use its discretion to treat similarly situated businesses and individuals differently. These opportunities for discrimination can be seen clearly both in the detection of the violation of rules and in the standards for enforcement.

Methods of Detection. In contrast with most executive branch agencies, the FCC has substantial discretion in how it chooses to detect wrongdoings by its licensees. One means of detecting violations of the many laws and rules for which it is responsible is to wait for a formal complaint. Thus, for example, the FCC does not monitor broadcast programming in the United States for indecency, but should a viewer or listener file a complaint, the commission may launch an investigation. Similarly, FCC wireless and broadcast licenses provide for specific use of the spectrum and noninterference from other sources. Many radio licensees complain both formally and informally about interference, but, as most are painfully aware, the FCC has limited resources to protect them from it and enforce their exclusivity rights. In any given year, only a small proportion of interference complaints are fully investigated. While protection of interference rights is much less than absolute, the system is generally perceived as "fair" to the extent that the method the FCC uses to determine which complaints to investigate is not predictably biased in favor of or against certain individual or particular categories of licensees.

Another form of detection is based on anonymous informal complaints. A company not wishing to annoy its business rival publicly may tattle to the FCC. The FCC may launch an informal investigation and, if it finds sufficient evidence of wrongdoing, may conduct a formal investigation, never publicly revealing the origin of the complaint. It is impossible to verify whether the FCC responds to informal complaints in a nondiscriminatory manner because, by definition, no records are kept of them. Informal, anonymous complaints as the basis of detection of wrongdoing give a government agency broad discretion that can easily be abused. For this reason, the absence of formal complaints in adjudicatory proceedings, such as the applications for Bell Operating Companies to offer long-distance services, is greeted with skepticism.[2]

A third form of detection is an investigation that is initiated by a government agency without first receiving a complaint. Random screening for compliance with rules is not necessarily discriminatory if it is truly random, or if there are clear standards to investigate one class of business more than another. Thus, airport security personnel may check some passengers more thoroughly than others based on randomness or discernible characteristics. The IRS in investigating tax returns has both random audits and audits triggered by unusual filing characteristics.

Given the amount of discretion involved, however, self-initiated enforcement actions can easily lend themselves to differential treatment of individuals, businesses, or certain classes of businesses. Such was the case with perhaps the most unusual instance of this kind of action by the FCC, involving property audits that later were dropped in the CALLS proceeding (discussed in detail below).

For years, the FCC has had detailed recordkeeping requirements for physical plant and equipment used by carriers for telecommunications services. These records were kept on an honor-system basis, with no FCC verification. In 1997, the FCC did something quite dramatic and unprecedented: It conducted, based on a sample of central offices, a surprise audit of the plant and equipment of major local telephone companies.[3] Some items of plant and equipment could not be instantaneously identified. Companies were not allowed to locate the missing plant and equipment, nor were they allowed to update their records. Based on the results from the sample of audited central offices, the FCC staff extrapolated across the entire universe of large local phone company plant and equipment to estimate that many billions of dollars' worth were missing.[4]

On closer inspection, it was hard to accept the audits as final. Claims of accounting fraud, particularly where billions of dollars are stake, are serious charges. The burden of proof for accurate recordkeeping is on the regulated carrier, not the FCC. But to substantiate its claims, the FCC should have encouraged and reviewed explanations of alleged missing plant and equipment, a process the agency seemed unwilling to permit. Many individuals, both inside and outside the FCC, raised the issue of the accuracy of the audits with the agency. The consistent response from inside the FCC was that, "of course," they were not accurate. More than one individual suggested that they were a "poker chip" to be played later in some intricate deal at the FCC.

As we will see, the "poker chip" was played in the CALLS proceeding. The enforcement of the audits was ostensibly dropped in exchange for concessions from major local telephone companies, although in practice the audits could never have withstood scrutiny.[5] The mixing of an enforcement procedure—usually a closed record—with a rulemaking, usually an open record, caused concerns for the treatment of company proprietary information from the audits.[6]

The actual meaning of the 1997 audits is shrouded in mystery. Because the proceeding was unceremoniously dropped, no one will ever know whether the large telephone companies were guilty of careless or even fraudulent bookkeeping, whether the FCC was careless in its audit procedures, or both.

The FCC had never conducted property audits before, and has not conducted such audits since. But in the way in which they were carried out, and the use to which the results were later put, these procedures suffered the appearance, if not the actuality, of discriminatory treatment of outside parties.

Standards of Enforcement. After a wrongdoing has been detected, most government agencies have predictable and nondiscriminatory standards of enforcement. Violations of some FCC rules, such as insufficient lighting on radio towers, have routine standards of enforcement. But in many instances, detection of wrongdoing leads to unpredictable and discretionary standards of enforcement.

At the extreme are the standards for enforcement of rules that do not even exist. In September 2000, less than two months before a presidential election, the FCC sent threatening letters to broadcast licensees concerning "subliminal" messages in an advertisement sponsored by the Republican National Committee; of course, the FCC had no rules on subliminal messages.[7] The matter was ultimately dropped, but the mere threat of enforcement of a nonexistent rule sent a chilling signal to FCC licensees. A licensee might reasonably wonder how it could avoid running afoul of a regulatory agency that threatens to enforce nonexistent rules, particularly ones with overt political overtones.

For several years after the passage of the Telecommunications Act of 1996, "slamming" provided another example of a violation of a nonexistent rule. "Slamming" is the unauthorized switching of long-distance carriers. While the Act forbids this reprehensible activity,[8] as of 1998 the commission had adopted no formal rules to implement these provisions.[9] Meanwhile, the FCC received numerous slamming complaints, both formal and informal, and brought enforcement actions against what, at the time, appeared to be some of the more egregious cases.[10]

The FCC subsequently wrote clear antislamming rules. In retrospect, however, its enforcement actions before rules were written were hardly above suspicion of being discriminatory. Many carriers were accused of slamming, but the FCC acted only against the most aggressive. These actions were made without any basis in rules, as no standards had been set to distinguish between aggressive marketing and unlawful activity.

The vast majority of administrative and enforcement decisions at the FCC follow predictable procedures. But it is the constant opportunity to use discretion, even if only occasionally employed, that leaves parties before the

FCC with a fear of discrimination. A purely enforcement agency would not likely have such wide-ranging discretion; its enforcement discretion would be limited by the rulemaking or adjudicatory decisions of the other branches of government. In each of the instances described above—the records audit, the threatening letters regarding subliminal ads, and the anti-slamming actions—its combined powers of government enabled the FCC to engage in discriminatory enforcement practices when it chose to do so.

Discriminatory Adjudicatory Proceedings

Disputes about the interpretation of legal rights are common. Government agencies hear and resolve these disputes through adjudicatory proceedings. Private parties look to the government to resolve disputes fairly, treating all similarly situated parties the same. Most courts can neither write laws nor enforce them. They satisfy themselves with adjudicating disputes between parties by merely *interpreting* the law, rather than *rewriting* it.

A conglomerated agency such as the FCC has an opportunity to transform an adjudicatory proceeding involving interpretations of existing rules into a rulemaking or enforcement proceeding for a specific company even where rules, much less enforcement, do not exist. The result is not just a concentration of powers but, often, company-specific laws, which by their very nature are discriminatory. Four examples at the commission are immediately apparent: merger reviews; applications of Bell Operating Companies to offer long-distance services; waivers; and the CALLS proceeding.

Merger Review Activities at the FCC. Every year, businesses, both large and small, merge for any number of reasons. The federal government has sophisticated antitrust laws to ensure that these mergers do not result in anticompetitive combinations. Two federal agencies, the Department of Justice's Antitrust Division and the Federal Trade Commission, enforce these laws with large professional staffs.

The FCC has no specific statutory authority to review mergers, except under the limited Clayton Act, an authority that apparently has never been exercised by the FCC.[11] Instead, the commission relies on the license transfer process under the Communications Act of 1934.[12]

Before 1996, major mergers in the communications sector were rare, often restricted by a range of regulations limiting ownership. The infrequent major transaction typically involved acquisition by a firm without substantially regulated assets.[13] FCC reviews of these transactions tended to focus on compliance with the existing burden of commission rules rather than on novel concepts of broader competition within the national economy, although even these reviews were certainly not frequent enough for the commission to develop merger review guidelines. None led to conditions placed by the FCC that went beyond preexisting agency rules.

The Telecommunications Act of 1996 unleashed decades of pent-up demand to better rationalize the structure of business organizations in the communications sector. The year 1996, with more than one hundred billion dollars' worth of announced mergers in the sector, saw a substantial increase in merger activity over prior years. The initial mergers after the Act tended to be reviewed upon the same narrow basis—often by bureaus on delegated authority rather than by the full commission—as the infrequent pre-Act mergers had been.[14]

The Bell Atlantic–NYNEX combination was the watershed merger that established a bold departure from precedent by the FCC to create company-specific laws in response to mergers.[15] In an aggressive order, one of the last major orders under Chairman Reed Hundt, the FCC dismissed the limitations of the Clayton Act and asserted a new "public interest" standard for the review of mergers that implicitly meant the FCC could impose any conditions for any reason on any merger.[16]

The process initiated by the FCC in the Bell Atlantic–NYNEX merger had the following steps:

- Avoid written rules about which mergers will be reviewed and what process will be followed.

- Transform the license transfer process into a means of finding "public interest" benefits to outweigh the harms or lack of benefits resulting from the merger.

- Seek wide-ranging comments in opposition to the merger from interested parties, at times even using public forums to attack it.[17]

- Delay approval of the license transfer.

- Articulate long-term conditions to create firm-specific rules that the FCC could not on its own lawfully impose on all such similarly situated firms.

- Compel the merging parties to "volunteer" to offer the conditions.

The merger review process initiated in the Bell Atlantic–NYNEX transaction stands in stark contrast to that used by the primary federal antitrust agencies, the DOJ and the FTC. Those agencies go to great lengths to avoid redundant review; one and only one agency will review a merger. The antitrust process is well established, following written guidelines with predictable interpretations, and it is carried out discreetly, rather than taking place in a public forum. The vast majority of mergers do not receive so much as a second review; a large number—but a small percentage—have negotiated consent decrees to divest in advance assets related to market power that might be created by the merger, rather than permanent regulatory obligations, and only a small number are actually challenged in court. The antitrust review is not a means of creating "public interest" benefits.

Technically, the FCC did not "approve" the Bell Atlantic–NYNEX merger only subject to "surprise" conditions on unwilling and unwitting parties; such a sequence would have led to a lengthy "hearing" process. Instead, the FCC negotiated with the merger parties in advance and made clear that, without the stipulated conditions, the merger, which had already languished for more than a year at the agency, would be delayed still longer.[18] The FCC imposed the negotiated conditions only on the newly merged Bell Atlantic—conditions that, if they had any merit, could not have been lawfully applied to the incumbent local exchange industry, much less a single firm. The merging parties were compelled to "volunteer" to offer the stipulated conditions and, in so doing, foreclosed most avenues for litigation appeal of them. In most areas of law, contracts entered under duress are not binding, but under administrative law, the condition of duress is rarely, if ever, argued.

The FCC never looked back to the detached form of merger reviews it had exercised before the Bell Atlantic–NYNEX transactions. Afterward, the detailed, "public interest" review became the norm rather than the exception.

Even without clear legal authority, the FCC invented a process confident that no one would challenge it;[19] and, as shown in the appendix, the vast majority of subsequent merger reviews by the full commission imposed conditions that went beyond the then-existing FCC rules.

From the perspective of an agency accumulating power, the Bell Atlantic–NYNEX merger was an unmitigated success. The form and substance of the conditions imposed by the FCC were far different from those an antitrust agency would have imposed. Whereas a private party before a purely executive branch agency might have challenged the discretionary use of power in court, in Congress, or in both, the newly merged Bell Atlantic did not challenge the outcome. Indeed, it would have had an awkward case, given that it had "volunteered" the conditions.

In 2000, Chairman Kennard created a formal "merger review team," with its own web location, within the Office of General Counsel.[20] The merger review team continued under Chairman Powell. Its Web site lists mergers under review but fails to describe the screening technique used to decide which mergers will be reviewed. Yet the mergers intensively reviewed by the FCC are only a small portion of all mergers, only a small portion of mergers within the communications sector, and only a small portion of all license transfers at the FCC.

Of course, in the exercise of its administrative authority, it would be entirely proper for the FCC to condition license transfers on compliance with FCC rules, and even to inspect closely whether the merging parties are in compliance with those rules. But compliance with existing rules rarely is the focus of FCC license transfer reviews. The merger reviews became examples of improper administrative behavior. The following is a list of the failings from just one merger review, SBC-Ameritech:

- The transaction was found to be out of compliance, even though it did not violate any extant statute or rule.

- The alleged harms were speculative and unrelated to the merger.

- The conditions did not remediate the alleged harms.

- The conditions were inconsistent with the Communications Act.

- The conditions were disproportionate to the alleged harms.

- The conditions placed undue administrative burdens and costs on both the FCC and participants in the telecommunications market.

- The conditions were either voluntary and therefore unenforceable or involuntary and therefore judicially reviewable.

- The FCC lacked merger-review authority.

- The order was adopted pursuant to extraordinary procedures that undermined the appearance of impartial decision-making.

- The order was adopted pursuant to an ad hoc and potentially arbitrary rule.

- The order failed to articulate intelligible principles for the "public interest" test for mergers.[21]

These and other failings are found in practically every merger reviewed by the FCC. The problems were so rampant that congressional hearings on the subject were held both by the House Judiciary Committee[22] and the House Commerce Committee.[23]

Some of the most egregious examples of policy exploits masquerading as merger reviews occur in the context of mass media license transfers. For example, Sinclair applied to transfer licenses from Sullivan Broadcast Holdings and from Glencairn on November 16, 1999.[24] Sinclair was not popular at the FCC, and so it was punished in the license transfer process, with some of its transfers contested on the basis of the FCC's new ownership attribution rules.[25] Sinclair filed for a writ of mandamus with the D.C. Circuit Court of Appeals on September 10, 2001, seeking to force the FCC to make a decision. The FCC subsequently decided on November 15, 2001, to grant all but one of the requested license transfers.[26] The agency issued a notice of apparent liability to Sinclair and Glencairn after finding that Sinclair had effectively controlled Glencairn licenses without seeking a transfer of control.[27]

In another case in 1997, Paxson Communications Corporation petitioned for transfer of control of one of the WQED Pittsburgh licenses.[28] After a long, contentious saga, the FCC in December 1999—more than two years after the initial application—ultimately granted the license transfer to PCC, but only after creating "guidance" for educational programming content.[29]

TABLE 9.1

MAJOR TRANSACTIONS LISTED AT THE MERGER REVIEW TEAM WEB SITE
FISCAL YEARS 1997–2002

	1997	1998	1999	2000	2001	2002
Major transactions listed	2	2	2	12	13	9
Commission approved with ad hoc conditions	1	1	2	8	3	2
Commission approved without ad hoc conditions	1	1	0	1	0	0
Bureau approved with ad hoc conditions	0	0	0	0	1	1
Bureau approved without ad hoc conditions	0	0	0	2	8	6
Withdrawn	0	0	0	1	1	0
Rejected or designated for hearing	0	0	0	0	0	0

SOURCE: Author's calculations. Table 9.1 includes only those designated by the FCC's merger review team as "major" or in its archives. See FCC, Office of General Counsel, Transaction Team, "Major Transaction Decisions," November 15, 2002, http://www.fcc.gov/transaction/mergerorderschron.html (accessed October 14, 2005). Major multibillion-dollar mergers not listed by the FCC include U.S. West–Continental Cable; Qwest–LCI; Time Warner–Turner Broadcasting; and MCI-MFS.
NOTE: Ad hoc conditions are conditions beyond those necessary to bring applicants into compliance with FCC rules.

The clear affront to the First Amendment caused the FCC to withdraw the guidance within six weeks.[30] The FCC demonstrated that it could take a long time to conduct a simple license transfer, and that it could create extraordinary regulatory costs by placing superfluous conditions on license transfers, in this case content regulation, in the process.

Table 9.1 lists the number of mergers by fiscal year and their disposition by the FCC, as listed at the merger review team Web site in late 2002. The sharp increase in FY 2000 simply reflects the date of the creation of the merger review team. Previously, mergers had been reviewed on a more ad hoc basis.

Some major mergers are reviewed by the full commission, and some on delegated authority are reviewed at the bureau level. The FCC has no clear rules to determine where a merger will be reviewed.[31] As can be seen in the table, most of those reviewed by the full commission are approved only with ad hoc conditions beyond those necessary to bring the merging parties into compliance with FCC rules. The net effect of these ad hoc merger conditions is company-specific rules and regulations. In contrast, major mergers reviewed by bureaus are unlikely to face conditions beyond what is necessary to bring the licensees into compliance.

Notice that none of the major mergers was disapproved—that is, designated for hearing—between FY 1997 and FY 2002. The first to be designated for hearing was the EchoStar-Hughes transaction, in FY 2003.

Of course, all of the mergers reviewed by the FCC, as listed in table 9.1, were also reviewed by either the FTC or the DOJ. It is never the case that the FCC reviews a major merger without a review by one of the federal antitrust agencies. The FCC review might make more sense if it were limited to issues related just to FCC rules or statutes, but few, if any, of the FCC reviews fail to mention antitrust and economic competition issues. Indeed, some seem entirely based on antitrust analysis.[32]

Moreover, many of the merger reviews in the period covered by the table involved what amounted to a "balancing" of additional doses of "public interest" to offset the harms associated with a merger. This balancing approach was properly decried by then-commissioner Michael Powell in several statements objecting to the merger process.[33] Under this approach, an underlying merger, no matter how harmful, can always be remedied by offsetting public interest contributions. Regrettably, the FCC appears to have continued and expanded the balancing review of public interest under Chairman Powell.[34]

Of course, not all major mergers are reviewed by the FCC. Table 9.2 lists some of the major mergers that have not been reviewed by the commission in recent years. In each instance, the merging parties held many FCC licenses, at times substantially exceeding those held by parties that were subject to review.

Throughout the periods covered by tables 9.1 and 9.2, the FCC generally refused to codify its merger review process, so as to preserve as much discretion for itself as possible. The agency's approach to the process remains extremely ad hoc. More than ten thousand license transfers are reviewed each year by the commission and submitted for public comment,[35] but few are designated as "major" by the merger review team.[36] Some of the transfers that

TABLE 9.2

MAJOR MERGERS FROM 1997 TO 2001 THAT WERE NOT
REVIEWED BY THE FCC

Exxon-Mobil	Dow Chemical–Union Carbide
Chevron-Texaco	El Paso Energy–Coastal Corporation
Georgia-Pacific–Fort James	SmithKline–Glaxo Wellcome
Pepsico-Quaker	Philip Morris–Nabisco Holdings
Tribune–Times Mirror	Pfizer–Warner Lambert
Citibank-Travelers	TV Guide–Gemstar
Hewlett Packard–Compaq	Daimler-Chrysler
Boeing–McDonnell Douglas	

SOURCE: Author's research.

are not designated as "major" receive comments, have conditions placed on the transfers, and may even have transfers designated for hearing. The net result is that many regulated entities before the FCC, particularly the larger companies, face rules that are peculiar to each company. Table 9.3 lists some of the businesses that face company-specific rules.

BOC Section 271 Reviews. Another instance in which the FCC engaged in discriminatory adjudication proceedings concerns section 271 BOC reviews between 1997 and 2003.[37] According to the 1996 Act, a Bell Operating Company (BOC) could offer interLATA (long-distance) services in a state only after the FCC reviewed its adherence to section 271.[38] The section is extremely detailed and, at first glance, not subject to substantial discretion. If those conditions were not met, a BOC could not offer services. The FCC was neither permitted to expand nor to contract the statutory provisions, and, presumably, treated BOCs the same way as any other companies seeking to offer the same services.[39]

In practice, the FCC applied section 271 by imposing ad hoc conditions on BOCs to meet the specific circumstances of each state. In each instance, the conditions went beyond the actual requirements of section 271. At the same time, the FCC did not uniformly attempt to resolve disputes over a BOC's compliance with other sections of the Act, as required by section 271.[40]

TABLE 9.3
MAJOR BUSINESSES FACING COMPANY-SPECIFIC RULES AT THE FCC

Telecommunications Companies	Media
SBC	AOL
Verizon	Viacom
BellSouth	General Electric
Qwest	NewsCorp
AT&T	Comcast
WorldCom	Clear Channel
	Practically every local ownership group

SOURCE: Author's research.

Thus, on the one hand, these conditions discriminated against a BOC applying under section 271, inasmuch as they required the BOC to engage in activities beyond those specifically required under the Act. On the other, they discriminated in favor of a BOC, inasmuch as the BOC seemingly substituted ad hoc conditions for noncompliance with other sections of the Act. In short, while the ad hoc conditions can be interpreted variously as favoring or harming the BOCs, they unambiguously undermine the authority of the Act, while bolstering the arbitrary discretion of the FCC to discriminate in favor of or against individual regulated entities.

Rather than simply determining whether BOCs met the requirements for offering long-distance services under the law, the FCC made all their section 271 applications subject to negotiations. The BOCs were willing to negotiate practically any terms to gain approval. Competing carriers informally provided heart-wrenching stories of unlawful acts by BOCs, but they would rarely file formal complaints, perhaps because such complaints were actively discouraged by both state and federal officials. Instead, competing companies were encouraged to participate in a "collaborative" process with BOCs, a touchy-feely set of negotiations at the state level to resolve issues in an informal setting.

It is easy to recognize "collaborative" processes as a means of circumventing formal complaint processes, and of allowing government officials to make unreviewable judgments on disputes between private parties. The beauty of it all was that there were no formal records, no bases for appeals, no clear lawful rules for how the entire operation worked. Many parties believed that these "collaborative" processes were efficient, but the result was company-specific proceedings that had no basis in the law.

The section 271 orders themselves, particularly the successful applications, were not remotely constructed from the law itself. Verizon's successful application in New York, the first, was based not on a narrow reading of the fourteen-point checklist of the law, but on thousands of confidence-building conditions not found there. In fact, the commission on this and on other applications never made an unambiguous finding for those elements of the checklist addressing compliance with certain subsections of sections 251 and 252.[41]

AT&T and others challenged the legality of the FCC's decision in New York, but on the wrong grounds. A strict statutory challenge of both the commission's negotiation process and the conditional outcome might have gained some traction. Instead, the D.C. Circuit affirmed the FCC's decision, not because it had strictly followed the law, but almost out of exasperation over how better to interpret section 271 when the petitioners had not provided a clearly more lawful alternative.[42]

This unfortunate precedent of negotiation and conditions outside the law became the accepted norm for all section 271 applications. The section 271 reviews were not clearly based on the law, and regulators at both the federal and state levels had newfound discretion over a major issue. Amazingly, with countless thousands of lawyers in the communications sector, none wrote a successful challenge to a very vulnerable section 271 process.

The negotiated settlements were not surprising. For decades, the FCC operated—and the states still operate—as regulator of a monopoly. It is the norm rather than the exception to negotiate outcomes. It is a cozy model that works well with a regulated monopoly, but is quickly dysfunctional with a competitive market.

Waivers. The FCC makes extensive and discriminatory use of waivers of its rules to individual regulated entities. Waivers are a useful tool for the agency when regulated entities have immediate problems that cannot be clearly resolved under then-existing FCC rules, yet rulemaking proceedings last for years. In recent years, the FCC, usually through bureaus on delegated authority, has granted countless waivers of its rules. Merger reviews are another common vehicle for the grant of waivers.

It is precisely because the grant of a waiver is both discretionary and common that many large, regulated entities have taken on the appearance of facing company-specific rules rather than general ones that apply to all similarly situated entities. The FCC does not always grant waivers, and when it does, it may give them different terms. For example, many mergers involving television broadcast licensees would bring the merging parties into direct violation of one or more of the FCC's many broadcast ownership rules. Rather than turn down all of the license transfers in its merger review process, the FCC grants "temporary" waivers of its rules to allow the merging parties to sell assets to bring the newly merged entity into compliance. The amount of time the FCC grants for the temporary waivers in major merger proceedings varies substantially. Similarly, during the pendency of the review of the local broadcast ownership rules in the 1990s, the FCC granted many waivers to its rules for local ownership groups.

The CALLS Proceeding. A case that exemplifies all of the various elements described above of the FCC's discriminatory behavior in enforcing and adjudicating the law is the CALLS proceeding, which will be described here in detail.

Telecommunications services are usually delivered over equipment belonging to more than one company. Complex financial arrangements determine how owners of equipment are paid for the use of, or access to, their assets in providing telecommunications services. For example, a two-minute telephone call from New York to Los Angeles may originate from a customer whose local service provider is Verizon. The call may be transferred to AT&T at a switch in New York. AT&T may then carry the call over its own network to Los Angeles, where it may be transferred to SBC's local network, through which one of SBC's own customers receives the call.

It is easy to see how paying for this call gets rather complicated. Before the dismantling of AT&T in the early 1980s, the payment went to one entity, which owned the entire network. Back then, AT&T, at the behest of federal and state regulators, charged rates well above its costs for long-distance calls, and used profits from those calls to subsidize residential and rural consumers. This system of implicit subsidies worked only in a monopoly environment where lower-priced competitors were prevented from entering the market.

The dismemberment of AT&T and the entry of new market participants resulted in multiple companies owning portions of the communications network, each of which requires compensation in order to maintain the assets it shares for use by the entire network. In a case like the New York–Los Angeles call described above, the long-distance carrier, in this instance AT&T, typically will send a bill for the call to the originating customer in New York and charge ten cents for the two-minute call. In turn, AT&T will pay a small fee to Verizon for originating access and another small fee to SBC for terminating access. These payments from long-distance carriers to local exchange carriers are commonly called interstate *access charges*. They are designed to compensate carriers for providing and maintaining the local portion of the telecommunications network that enables customers to access the interstate network connecting New York, Los Angeles, and any place in between.

Immediately after divestiture, interstate access charges were both large and heavily regulated by the FCC. Over time, they have declined, and regulatory review has evolved to little more than the posting of a tariff. Yet interstate access charges have always been a source of dispute between local and long-distance companies. The former want higher interstate access charges, while the latter want lower charges, or even no charges at all.

For many years in the 1980s and '90s, interstate access charges were regulated based on complex rate-of-return calculations for that portion of the local network costs attributed to support interstate services. In turn, state regulators excluded the portion of the local network assigned to intrastate purposes from the asset base used in their own rate-of-return calculations determining regulated local rates. All of these regulatory calculations to allocate fixed costs to jointly provided services were entirely arbitrary and a great waste of time. Regulators nonetheless went to great lengths to calculate interstate access charges down to precise fractions of a penny, a tribute to the regulatory penchant to be precisely wrong rather than approximately right.

Practically everyone in the industry knew that the interstate access charge regime was unsustainable. Wireless services managed to negotiate their own access arrangements without the "help" of regulators, eventually delivering rates so low that they were able to take market share away from the dedicated long-distance companies. At the same time, artificially high interstate access charges for landline services encouraged large corporations to set up their own private networks, effectively bypassing the regulated switched system with all its access charges. Finally, the Internet developed an inexpensive alternative for calls that threatened to displace domestic interstate service with effectively free calls.

In 1999, the FCC, frustrated by a long list of complaints by local and long-distance companies—two groups that were pitted against each other under the commission's regulatory regime—began to consider the reregulation of long-distance rates, particularly the fixed monthly charges paid by residential customers.[43] The FCC had recently reduced interstate access charges paid to local exchange carriers and increased universal service payments at the same time.[44] Now it considered taking additional, similar steps.[45]

One solution would have been to separate the various issues and write rules for each, but a group of large telephone companies called the Coalition for Affordable Local and Long Distance Service ("CALLS") proposed that the FCC solve all of these conflicting problems in one fell swoop.[46]

The CALLS coalition consisted of two large long-distance companies (AT&T and Sprint), as well as several large incumbent telephone companies (Bell Atlantic, GTE, BellSouth, Ameritech, and SBC). Not all large companies participated in CALLS; WorldCom and U.S. West were dissatisfied with the CALLS agenda and noticeably absent. In addition, thousands of smaller carriers, both local and long-distance, did not participate.

Under the CALLS proposal, long-distance carriers would pay dramatically lower interstate access charges. To compensate local carriers for the loss of revenues, they would receive a higher federal monthly fee from consumers called a "subscriber line charge." In addition, large incumbent carriers would receive a new, company-specific, universal service fund of approximately $650 million. Of course, the entire premise of high-cost universal service support was to ensure delivery of telecommunications services in rural and high-cost areas, while the lion's share of lost access-charge revenues was to come from large urban areas.

The CALLS proposal was an example of "fairness" engineered with company-specific rules. These included imposition of company-specific universal service payments, enforcements, and adjudication proceedings. Moreover, the CALLS proposal only applied to large, incumbent local companies and large interexchange carriers. Small companies were to be left out.

The creation of a $650 million annual universal service fund targeted only at large telecommunications carriers, the increases in the fee structure and taxes to support it, and the substantial increase in the subscriber line charge were clearly rulemaking exercises. The selection of a cost model to distribute the $650 million annual fund to some companies rather than others was a political judgment that perhaps required legislative authority not typically delegated to regulatory rulemakers. The selection of a computer cost model that took approximately 180 hours to run, yielding results that changed during many early runs, was an exercise in regulatory hubris. It was obvious that the model would not work.[47] Reasonable people believed that the FCC favored the CALLS proposal not for its computational elegance, but for the opening it gave the FCC to collect and distribute another $650 million.

As embarrassing as the conflicting tradeoffs entailed in the original CALLS proposal were, they were perfectly innocuous in comparison with both the process and the decisions that ultimately followed. Much of the FCC was intrigued by the original proposal, but some of the suggestions—such as substantially higher subscriber line charges to compensate the incumbent local exchange carriers for lost access charges—ran against the general drift of then-prevailing FCC policy, which favored lower, not higher, fixed charges for residential consumers. The FCC had recently released a Notice of Inquiry to explore lower fixed charges for residential long-distance customers.[48]

Rather than divide the CALLS proposal into its separate parts and consider each individually, the FCC embarked on months of negotiations over the larger "deal." These negotiations were conducted privately with the members of the CALLS coalition. While many other parties wanted to participate, most were excluded.[49] To ameliorate the large independent local exchange carriers (ILECs) for not getting quite as much compensation from higher subscriber line charges as they had hoped, the FCC negotiated at least three issues of interest to them:

- a new rulemaking proceeding limiting the obligations of incumbent local exchange carriers to lease facilities to their competitors;[50]

- a separate rulemaking proceeding that involved forbearance on depreciation schedules for ILEC equipment, initially rejected by the FCC[51] and then reconsidered;[52] and

- an enforcement and adjudicatory proceeding that involved the resolution of the continuing property record audits (discussed earlier in this chapter).[53]

Of course, no written record of the private negotiations with the FCC survives, but apparently the deal involved concessions to the ILECs on each of these three issues in exchange for ILEC concessions on the initial proposal, particularly subscriber line charges. The private negotiations were completed in early 2000, and CALLS modified its proposal and resubmitted it to the FCC.[54] Left unstated were implicit agreements, perhaps including the eventual dropping of the continuing property record audits. In short order, the FCC adopted the provisions of the revised proposal.[55]

The FCC's private negotiating process in the CALLS proceeding was almost certainly unlawful, both for its lack of transparency and for its commingling of information from disparate and unrelated proceedings, some of them closed adjudicatory proceedings. There is a lawful method to have publicly negotiated at least the rulemaking components of the CALLS proposal—for example, the FCC has rules for the submission and review of comments, or ex parte rules—but that was not followed.[56] Parties that were not part of the coalition had little meaningful input. The entire modified proposal was a *fait accompli* from the moment it was introduced; it sailed through the FCC in a matter of a few months, a record for such a complicated rulemaking.[57]

U.S. West, which was not a part of the coalition and which received few, if any, of the new universal service funds under the FCC's opaque universal service model, challenged the entire proceeding in court. At the same time, Qwest was acquiring U.S. West. As part of the review of the transaction, representatives of Qwest came to visit the FCC and present their case.

The new management of Qwest clearly saw value in maintaining good relations with the FCC, in contrast with U.S. West's confrontational approach. Although Qwest had not reviewed the case in detail, its inclination was to avoid offending the FCC. If the case were scaled back or even dropped, there would be no doubt that Qwest would win approval of its acquisition. Qwest did pursue two pieces of litigation related to the CALLS proceeding, but neither threatened the overall process.[58]

No party appears to have filed against the peculiarities of the entire administrative process under the CALLS decision: the ex parte rules, the transparent quid pro quo of dropping an enforcement action in exchange for rulemaking and an adjudication in unrelated matters, the use of universal service mechanisms to compensate companies for lost revenues in low-cost urban areas, and many other irregularities. At the end of the CALLS proceeding, the FCC had once again succeeded in creating a set of company-specific rules. The threat of property audits served the FCC as an intimidating stack of poker chips in a high-stakes game known as "CALLS."

The adjustment of company-specific, regulated access charges in the CALLS case was a form of adjudication. The entire premise of the original CALLS proposal was a train wreck of legislative, enforcement, and adjudicatory authority.[59] The unbridled combination of legislative, executive, and judicial authority at the FCC reached its destructive heights in the CALLS proceeding, with the agency using private meetings to shield itself from the public to negotiate tradeoffs among rulemakings, enforcement actions, and adjudications. A group of agencies operating in accordance with separation of powers could not have countenanced this process, much less reached its result.

The combination of powers at the FCC led to discriminatory company-specific proceedings affecting rules, enforcements, and adjudications related to the implementation of the 1996 Act. Private parties excluded from the CALLS proceeding were frightened to object too loudly. The other branches of government never heard about, or turned a blind eye to, the CALLS proceeding. But, as we shall see in the following chapter, the FCC and its combination of powers can reach discriminatory outcomes even when the other branches are actively engaged.

10

The Miracle of Compound Interests

An agency such as the FCC with the combined powers of government can more easily make discriminatory, company-specific administrative decisions than an agency with the powers of only one branch of government. The opportunity to make such decisions is the result of the combination of powers itself, not because other branches of government are unaware of the FCC's actions. Consider the case of NextWave, a wireless company whose administrative disputes with the FCC were closely monitored by the administration, Congress, and the courts.

The story of NextWave begins with FCC licenses to use spectrum. Without coordinated or restricted entry, the airwaves could become a cacophony of noise, useless to anyone. That was the fear, warranted or not, in the 1920s when radio stations could broadcast on any frequency. Rather than allow property rights through common law, the federal government interceded, claimed the rights to all spectrum, and began issuing licenses, for purposes the government alone would determine, to individuals the government alone would choose.

Since taking control of the spectrum in the 1920s, the government has assigned licenses to private parties in different manners. Some, such as amateur radio licenses, are not limited or scarce; they are assigned to anyone who wants one and can pass a test. For most other types of licenses, far more individuals apply than there are licenses to assign. The very scarcity of licenses creates value.

Historically, how did the FCC choose among competing applicants to assign a license? In earlier decades, the agency relied mostly on two means: comparative hearings and lotteries. Neither of these techniques was both efficient and fair. In the early 1990s, Congress decided to give the FCC the means to assign licenses more efficiently: the authority to assign them by auction. In the Omnibus Budget Act of 1993, it provided the FCC with a precise plan for carrying out these auctions by carefully crafting section 309(j), one of the longest and most convoluted subsections of the Communications Act of 1934. The result was a case study in how the FCC could use the combined powers of government to promote changing policy positions, even after losing in court.

Auctions

The FCC embraced the auction venture with great enthusiasm and, as in so many other instances, it began by using its legislative authority to "improve" upon Congress's instructions. From 1994 through 1996, the FCC generated a variety of notices and orders, tuning the implementation of these auctions as if that were the way to choose the best audience for their reception. They equipped "designated entities"—small or minority-owned businesses and rural telephone companies—with certain advantages to participate in auctions, and permitted small down payments and installment payments for the licenses.[1]

The auctions got off to an inauspicious start under these rules. Substantial problems were encountered in 1994, when winners of the first "interactive video and data service" (IVDS) auction failed to make good on their bids. The FCC's response was to use its enforcement authority to declare missed IVDS installment payments "suspended." Over the next five years it would resume them, then suspend them again, then intermittently repeat the process, leading to distress for the licensees and a general uncertainty that the agency's decisions were ever final.

Far worse were the results of subsequent auctions for licenses for commercial mobile radio services (CMRS). In 1995 and 1996, the FCC held a series of these auctions, many of which were labeled with a "block" name. The first two, the A-block and B-block auctions, were unmitigated successes. For these, the so-called personal communications services (PCS) auctions, winning bids were collected in full and licenses issued promptly.

Things changed with the C-block auction, scheduled for 1995. As with earlier auctions, the FCC had set aside a large section of spectrum—the C block—for designated entities. Not long before companies could sign up to participate, however, the Supreme Court declared in *Adarand v. Pena* that it had reservations about the structure of such set-asides. From then on, the government would have to prove that pertinent markets for government contracting services had exhibited an historical pattern of discrimination before these markets could be subjected to a correcting interference.[2]

Many concluded that the FCC would have to perform a costly and time-consuming *Adarand* study of the commercial mobile services market. Furthermore, a competent *Adarand* study might not find an historical pattern of discrimination, given that this market was new. In late 1995, the FCC obviated the *Adarand* study by collapsing the various qualifications that entitled such classes to designated-entity status into one—that of small business—thus finessing the issue of woman and minority ownership. Here the FCC used its constitutionally anomalous rulemaking authority to circumscribe the constitutional weakness of the statute. It was a precursor of things to come.

Peculiar Financing

In addition to limiting some auctions to designated entities, the FCC used its broad rulemaking authority to compensate for a perceived weakness in financial markets.[3] Ordinarily, when a company makes a large purchase, it arranges a line of credit to be available at closing. The FCC considered these customary commercial means of payments for large transactions and rejected them, arguing that small enterprises needed different means of getting into the telecommunications industry. The agency permitted winning bidders to pay the government for their licenses on an installment basis. Five percent would be due after the auction; another five percent would be due upon issuance of the license. After that, only low, interest-only payments would be due for the first few years. The FCC's lending venture was intended to help small businesses, but it likely had the opposite effect.

Practically the entire structure of the FCC's designated entity program was outside the clearest reading of the law. The FCC used its rulemaking authority to interpret the Communications Act imaginatively. The purpose of the installment payments was anything but regulatory in the sense of being related to FCC concerns about the operational behavior of a licensee under Title III of the Communications Act. The FCC had become a banker.

In retrospect, it is easy to criticize the FCC's initial rules for auctions in general and installment payments in particular. They were written expansively by the FCC, with a preoccupation of getting licenses into only the hands the commission deemed proper, rather than simply putting them into private hands that could then buy and trade them to put them to higher use. As such, the rules betrayed a misapprehension about the function of markets, a concern that markets would not achieve the "right" results, and a belief that careful tweaking by the FCC could make the world a better place.

Between 1994 and 1999, the FCC held dozens of spectrum auctions. It learned from each successive auction and tried to correct the mistakes of the past. For practically each auction, the FCC had new bidding rules, new designated entity rules, and new financing rules. Formal rules were written in the Code of Federal Regulations; informal rules were given by FCC staff. Both could change during the course of an auction, and legal uncertainty was everywhere.

It is impossible to review FCC auction documents related to designated entity programs between 1994 and 1996 without a clear sense that the agency was well aware of the risks of overbidding, financial default, and missed payments presented by the use of installment payments. The FCC went ahead with installment payments not because it was unaware of the risks they presented, but because it was all too aware of them, and thought the potential benefits of opening up licenses to small businesses outweighed them.

The C Block

Participation in the C-block auction was restricted to small businesses. Payments were to be made under the generous terms of an FCC-devised installment plan. Deposits to qualify for participation were due at the beginning of December 1995, well after the lessons of the IVDS debacle should have been learned by the FCC. Many companies, many of them newly formed, chose to participate in the C-block auction.

The auction formally commenced on December 18, 1995. The bidding rounds did not end until May 6, 1996, nearly five months later. When the C-block auction began, the disaster of the IVDS auction had already been revealed. Installment payments had been frozen by the FCC; the entire auction was in shambles. In a triumph of hope over experience, the FCC proceeded as if its failed IVDS scheme of providing easy financing for the highest bidder would work for the C block. Perhaps it was thought that IVDS licensees were just little mom-and-pop operations that had invested tens of thousands of dollars of personal assets in slivers of spectrum, and were too inexperienced in running a real telecommunications business to succeed. The C-block auction would be for real small businesses, investing millions of dollars in larger blocks of spectrum.

Despite official assertions to the contrary, in December 1995 and for the duration of the C-block auction it was difficult to take too seriously the FCC's warnings that this time it would stick to its guns and insist on prompt payments for licenses it would deliver in a timely manner. The C-block licenses did clearly state that they were conditional on payment; however, even at the time of the auction, the FCC was not threatening forfeiture for late payment. Indeed, the FCC's subsequent restructuring of the C-block auction in 1998 would have little meaning if the licenses disappeared with late payments.

Dozens of companies won C-block licenses. The three largest auction winners happened to be newly formed companies: NextWave, GWI, and Pocket Communications. Bids netted more than $10 billion of IOUs, of which more than $4 billion was promised by NextWave. After the auction, the winners expected to receive their licenses within a matter of weeks. That had been the experience of the larger companies in the A- and B-block auctions. There was no reason to expect the C-block results would be any different.

But they were. Some auction winners received their licenses in September 1996, four months after the auction finished. Others, such as NextWave, waited as long as nine months. For companies in precarious financial condition and facing rapidly fluctuating valuations, such delays could prove fatal.

Meanwhile, the FCC commenced other auctions, including the D, E, and F blocks. The commission continued to use its rulemaking authority to improve upon the results of its auctions. Each was slightly different from the one before it. Unfortunately, with auctions beginning every few months, it was impossible to correct problems that would take many months or even years to surface. Some flaws went undetected too long ever to be corrected.

On March 31, 1997, the FCC again abused a transitive verb, "suspending" quarterly interest payments on C- and F-block license winners, barely one month after NextWave received its C-block licenses, and less than three months after the conclusion of the F-block auction. It was the same fate that befell the IVDS auction, despite the FCC's various fixes to its payment financing schemes. The FCC had concluded several auctions, and had come to the sudden realization that its role as lender was a big mistake.

From late 1997 through early 1999, the general view of the C-block auction was that the successful bidders under the installment payment plan had simply bid "too much," or more than prevailing market valuations of wireless licenses could support. Had the FCC relied on the debt and capital markets to assume this critical valuation role from the beginning, imposing a market-based discipline on the bidding levels, this calamity could have been avoided. The FCC had assumed its knowledge was superior to the market and accepted bids paid with money it printed on its own presses. At this point, the prevailing view in government and the FCC was that the commission must find a way to get the auction winners to pay some of what they had bid, salvaging something from this wreck, regardless of market valuations, in order to maintain the fiction that the winning bids represented real valuations that the U.S. Treasury would one day realize. The FCC would use its enforcement and adjudicatory powers to that end to compensate for the failures of the rules for its installment payment schemes.

A New FCC—Where There's a Will There Must Be a Way

Four new FCC commissioners took office in November of 1997. From the start, the new commission gave every indication of being more forgiving of the C-block auction winners than had the previous one. But if there was a consistent thread in the early decisions of this new commission, it was the desire to extract as much money as possible out of this situation. Consider the case of Carolina PCS, a C-block auction winner that had failed to make its initial down payment in a timely manner, and thus had been denied its license by the Wireless Bureau of the FCC. The Wireless Bureau refused to grant Carolina PCS a waiver. In one of its first decisions as a commission, the new FCC, using its adjudicatory authority on Christmas Eve, 1997, reversed the Wireless Bureau decision and granted a waiver to Carolina PCS.[4] The FCC simply wanted some money for the license.

In March 1998, the commission staff worked out a negotiated settlement with Pocket Communications, whereby its bid was reduced by 60 percent, and terms of its payment were extended over twelve years.[5] There was no discussion of license forfeiture or turning over what was effectively a bankruptcy to a proper bankruptcy court. Again, the FCC used its adjudicatory authority to try to force Pocket to pay at least something for the licenses. The amount of funds that would come from Pocket Communications was now recognized as being something closer to the level supported by market conditions in 1998.

On April 24, 1998, a bankruptcy court in Texas handling the GWI bankruptcy case reached a very different conclusion. It found that the auction had been a fraudulent conveyance to GWI and relieved GWI of payment. The FCC was dismayed by the court decision, and on June 8, 1998, Chairman Kennard issued a statement praising the Department of Justice for appealing it.[6] Moreover, Kennard called on Congress to clarify the law. The clarification sought was not that licenses should be canceled when installment payments were in default, or that those communications laws pertaining to spectrum license auctions should override bankruptcy law; rather, Kennard simply sought clarification that "bankruptcy should not be used to hold auctioned licenses captive."[7] At the very least, the law was vague on the status of FCC licenses in bankruptcy court. Quite possibly, it was squarely on the side of providing bankruptcy protection for the defaulting bidder.

The same day, NextWave filed for bankruptcy protection and filed a fraudulent conveyance claim against the federal government. For much of the next year, the FCC's agenda on NextWave appeared to be avoiding a repeat of the GWI fiasco. The government's posture suggested an acceptance of bankruptcy law, through acknowledgements that the licenses were afforded bankruptcy protection, but in late 1998, the Wireless Bureau issued a statement purporting that installment payments were still due, even for licensees operating under bankruptcy protection.[8] This was an ambitious claim that did not carry the imprimatur of the full commission; however, it unambiguously asserted that licenses would be unilaterally voided if a licensee filed for bankruptcy and discontinued payments.

The FCC used its legislative authority to write the rules for auctions, including installment payments, exercised its administrative authority to conduct the auctions and seek installment payments, and selectively employed its adjudicatory authority to grant waivers and hear individual pleadings to compensate for earlier FCC errors. If these powers had been separated in different agencies, the inherent conflicts of responsibilities and interests the FCC enjoys and suffers from would not have given it so much rope with which to hang itself.

The Market Turns

The view of the C-block auction changed radically in 1999 as the public equity values of wireless companies turned upward. Many companies saw their stock prices increase several hundred percent in just a few months. There were at least three different reasons for this increase in valuations. One was that the value of telecommunications carriers went up generally, even outside of the wireless sector. They rose markedly in 1999. Second, stock prices of wireless carriers in other countries—such as Vodaphone, Orange, and Mannesmann—did particularly well in 1999, marking a worldwide increase in wireless carrier valuations. Third, mergers and acquisitions activity in the United States signaled a further future increase in the value of U.S. wireless properties. Merger and acquisition activity does not go up unless acquirers anticipate an increase in valuations.

Increasing valuations of large wireless companies made access to spectrum a growing concern. Large companies anticipated a need for more spectrum to expand existing voice services and to develop new services, such as high-speed data services. Companies could only obtain this spectrum by buying licenses from others, perhaps competitors, if the FCC did not make more spectrum available through the auction process. Despite laws requiring such efforts be undertaken, several FCC auctions were delayed indefinitely, beginning in 1999. These delays effectively added a scarcity premium to spectrum license valuations.

Eureka!

In 1999, these frothy spectrum valuations pointed industry and the FCC to a startling discovery: Perhaps the C- and F-block auction winners had bid *too little* for those licenses still languishing in bankruptcy courts. It turned out that the C-block licenses were exactly what large wireless service providers were looking for: large blocks of spectrum contiguous to spectrum they were currently using. It was perfect for adding capacity to existing lines of service.

How could a wireless carrier acquire some or all of the C-block licenses tied up in bankruptcy court? The simplest approach would be to acquire the bankrupt company, pay off its debts, and take over the licenses. But the transfer of FCC licenses, even in bankruptcy court, would require the approval of the FCC. Most of the licenses in bankruptcy court had restrictive covenants or conditions based on their assignment to designated entities. These conditions were based on rules that limited transferability to other designated entities or imposed penalties on transfers to other than designated entities. The rules were vague and frequently changing, such that the exact contours depended on staff and commissioner interpretations, often on a case-by-case basis.

Large wireless service providers made inquiries around the FCC to see if there were any methods for them to acquire valuable C-block licenses. Nextel tried negotiating an arrangement with FCC's Office of General Counsel, but not with the FCC itself, to acquire all of the NextWave licenses. Moribund companies in bankruptcy, such as NextWave, realized there might be real value in the assets they were still hanging onto.

The FCC attempted to satisfy the large wireless carriers without benefiting the C-block auction winners. Based on a theory that the licenses never should have been pulled into bankruptcy proceedings in the first place, the FCC might simply revoke the licenses of defaulting bidders and put them back up for auction, this time to an unrestricted group, including large companies. The chief obstacle to this plan was that it would require the FCC to backtrack on the legal position it had so far taken in bankruptcy courts. Using the commission's own original legal strategy against it, the bankrupt licensees might pursue litigation to keep the

FCC's hands off their licenses, which the agency had sold to them with full knowledge of their inability to finance them themselves.

The series of notices and orders that established the installment payment program spoke to issues of default of payment and bankruptcy in a way that forecast a case-by-case treatment by the FCC, rather than automatic license cancellation in event of payment default or bankruptcy. Automatic cancellation was perhaps indicated in the licenses; however, these provisions were never unequivocally or uniformly enforced. Indeed, the orders contemplated in some detail transfer of licenses by companies operating under bankruptcy protection that were supposed to be making installment payments.[9] Not until 1999 and 2000 did FCC orders assume automatic forfeiture of licenses without the possibility of administrative review in the event that a payment was missed.

The FCC's role as arbitrator of communications rules did not give it privilege in determinations of bankruptcy proceedings. The FCC would be forced to fall back on its invented role of creditor, something squarely outside of communications law, in order to justify its claims.

One of the mistakes the FCC made in auctions was using its rulemaking authority to become a lender, something that is not a specific duty or obligation of the FCC under the Communications Act of 1934. Yet throughout the legal wrangling over the C-block auction, the FCC never took the position that the installment payment program was anything other than a lending operation in which the agency was the sole creditor. In bankruptcy court, it initially assumed the role of creditor but later tried to recharacterize its role as "regulator."

Even if the FCC had explicit lending authority, it does not follow that it could condition the grant of licenses on that authority. It makes little sense to allow the FCC to condition licenses on performance of an activity that is not clearly part of the Communications Act. Had the two activities of license sales and license purchase financing been separated, as they would be in normal commercial circumstances, the lender's problem with the bankrupt borrower would not be an issue for the seller, who had been satisfied at closing by collection of its payment. If the FCC were able to condition licenses on the commission's invented role as creditor, then it could condition licenses on practically any imaginable activity it chose to associate with its regulatory role.

Regulatory vs. Fiduciary

How did the FCC find itself with the vast majority of C-block licenses tied up in bankruptcy proceedings? Was the FCC that organized the C-block auction staffed by grossly incompetent individuals and led by demonic commissioners who willfully or negligently proceeded to make mistake after mistake? Of course not. The commissioners and staff became trapped in a conflict between the commission's natural administrative role as license regulator and the unnatural role as lender that it legislated for itself. As regulator, the commission is indifferent to the identity or financial circumstances of licensees. It merely wants to see spectrum put to use without unlawful interference. To know and care about the identity and financial circumstances of licensees is an invitation for the commission to discriminate unlawfully among licensees.

On the other hand, the role of lender is precisely to be concerned about the identity and financial circumstances of loan recipients. It is the lender's fiduciary responsibility to discriminate between the creditworthy and those who are not. It is the lender's responsibility to peek behind the corporate veil, to ask about financial matters unrelated to regulated activities, to pry where a regulator dare not lawfully look. The regulator governs on a public record with open processes; the creditor operates on a private and confidential basis. These two roles are irreconcilable.

Former chairman Hundt believed that regulatory duty trumped fiduciary duty, and he cast blame in many directions. But his poetic observations were all too accurate:

> For ten months I have been stating that the key policy goal in wireless is competition, not debt collection. However, it is also true that this Commission, as a creditor, ought to behave in a commercially responsible manner. In America debtors who cannot pay are not thrown in prison, nor ought they be consigned to a Serbonian bog of Commission deliberations in which armies of lawyers and lobbyists and Commission staff are sunk. Yet for almost a year my colleagues on this Commission have been unwilling to make a commercially reasonable restructuring proposal of any kind to the financially troubled C-block

licensees. Nor have they been willing to promote competition by expediting some solution to the need to restructure and finance the C block.[10]

For decades, FCC licensees have bounced in and out of bankruptcy courts without the slightest concern to the FCC. These licensees were in bankruptcy court not because of debts owed to the FCC, but because of debts owed to third parties.

Typically, parties in bankruptcy court are seeking to make the most value out of a difficult situation. Only *interested* parties, those with claims on the assets of the party in bankruptcy, have standing in bankruptcy court. When a regulatory agency such as the FCC becomes a party to a bankruptcy proceeding, it is difficult to limit its role when it is also a part-time, moonlighting creditor.

The FCC has an administrative role as regulator. And it has a legislative role in writing rules to bring more spectrum into the public domain. In the latter capacity, it hears public comments, including those of firms that may have competing claims in a bankruptcy proceeding.

Collateral Damage

A change in legal position, particularly for a large public institution such as the FCC, is not an easy matter. Government agencies must make consistent arguments in different courts. A major change in legal position in one case may inadvertently affect legal positions in a wide range of other cases as well.

As the FCC's new strategy took hold in 1999, its legal position in practically every case became contorted by its position in the NextWave litigation. Every legal issue, at one time or another, had to pass through the NextWave litigation strategy test: Was the FCC's position in a particular matter consistent with the positions taken in NextWave? How would the FCC position in another litigation matter affect the NextWave proceedings? The obsession carried over into what seemed to be unrelated matters.

Changing federal government legal positions are costly not just to the government and opposing parties directly engaged with each other in litigation; they may be costly to other private parties as well—parties that might suffer what could be called collateral damage. Consider the case of Airadigm.

Partly owned by the Oneida Nation in Wisconsin, Airadigm won C-block licenses for spectrum in Wisconsin and Iowa and then followed Pocket Communications, GWI, NextWave, and other C-block bidders into bankruptcy after failing to make payments. Airadigm had more operational success than many other C-block bidders. It was able to build out part of its network, sign up thousands of customers, and offer service, even after it filed for bankruptcy protection and failed to make payments to the FCC. Airadigm and the Oneida Nation received a wink and a nod from the FCC that the agency would not try to reclaim their licenses.

In 2000, Airadigm found an opportunity to emerge from bankruptcy and bail out the Oneida tribe by selling its licenses. As with all transfers of FCC licenses, the commission would have to approve this transaction. Ordinarily, a license transfer benefiting a small company owned by an Indian tribe would be a routine affair. Unfortunately, letting Airadigm's sale go through would be contrary to the position the FCC had taken in the Second Circuit Court case: that the C-block licenses were invalid when a six-month grace period that followed a missed payment expired. Granting this license transfer would provide valuable ammunition to NextWave in its appellate litigation against the FCC. When choosing between helping both a Native American tribe and NextWave or helping itself, the FCC chose itself.

This was a very awkward situation for the FCC. Typically, the commission is extremely sensitive to and supportive of the needs of Native American tribes. So, instead of permitting an immediate license transfer, it instructed staff to find enough differences between NextWave and Airadigm situations to give it a plausible legal excuse for disparate treatment of these two parties.

Here was a small company, providing service to thousands of customers, simply trying to survive. It played by the rules as best it could. It wanted to sell its assets to another company, but the FCC would not let the sale go through. The FCC did not want to harm Airadigm, but it was so obsessed with getting NextWave out of its way that if Airadigm were to suffer for that, so be it. Airadigm's sale had to wait for years until the NextWave litigation was resolved.

Airadigm was lucky relative to another C-block auction winner, South-East Telephone Company. A small rural telephone company serving an impoverished corner of Appalachia, SouthEast happened to be located in the Kentucky congressional district of Hal Rogers, then chairman of the appropriations subcommittee having jurisdiction over the FCC. Despite his repeated efforts to help a constituent company, the FCC demonstrated to Rogers that the FCC would not be directly disciplined by Congress, not even by the chairman of a powerful committee.

SouthEast used its C-block licenses to offer wireless service in its local franchise. In late 1998, the FCC denied applications from Airadigm and SouthEast, as well as four other companies, for extensions of the date on which they were to resume their C-block license payments.[11] The FCC had not been convinced of a need for relief. SouthEast asked the commission to reconsider its decision, but it reached the same result in March 1999.[12] By that date, SouthEast's licenses had been voided, but the company, an otherwise solvent business, was not afforded the protection of bankruptcy court.

The second decision to deny SouthEast relief may well have been influenced by the NextWave litigation. By that time, giving SouthEast more time would have undermined the credibility of the commission's arguments in *NextWave v. FCC*. To add insult to the injury, the Wireless Bureau fined SouthEast for providing wireless services after its licenses to do so had been revoked. The size of the penalty was eventually reduced, but it was nevertheless imposed in order to shore up the FCC's case against NextWave. SouthEast paid the penalty. Airadigm, in the same situation, had not yet been forced to pay a penalty for operating under conditions the FCC described as being without a license.

Re-auction

Meanwhile, throughout 1999 and 2000, the FCC and NextWave continued to fight for control of the C- and F-block licenses in courtrooms in New York and Washington. The case bounced back and forth from one courtroom to another. In 2000, the Second Circuit found that communications law trumped bankruptcy law in this particular matter, a scary proposition given the unmapped and unpredictable idiosyncrasies of the former in contrast to the relatively clear precedents of the latter. This finding permitted the FCC to revoke licenses of companies that had defaulted on their installment payments. Following past practice, the agency then used its adjudicatory and enforcement powers to discriminate among different licensees, revoking some licenses while leaving others in place. Only the chosen were faced with a new round of government-funded litigation directed against them.

Even though a substantial shadow of doubt loomed over the ultimate outcome of litigation surrounding these revoked or forfeited licenses, the FCC took a further step and attempted to put them back up for auction. This was something any unscrupulous used car dealer would do, having repossessed what he'd just sold to a financially inexperienced customer who happened to miss a payment.

The FCC included the reclaimed NextWave licenses in a re-auction, called Auction 35, in December 2000 and January 2001. While much of the nation was glued to television sets watching the Florida recount debacle, the FCC was busily creating a legal nightmare of its own.

The most contentious issue was whether Auction 35 would be an open or invitational type of contest. While the reclaimed licenses from the C- and F-block auctions had originally been set aside for small businesses, most of the demand for them would come from the much larger companies that could actually pay for them. Comments before the FCC were divided on the issue of who should be allowed to submit bids. Some wanted the small-business restrictions of the first C- and F-block auctions to remain effective. Others wanted the auction opened up to all parties. The FCC resolved the dispute by opening some licenses to all bidders while reserving others for small businesses. Faced with a choice of an open or invitational format, the FCC chose a scramble.

The auction itself had been challenged by NextWave before the D.C. Circuit Court. NextWave sought an emergency stay in late 2000 pending the outcome of its case there. In arguments before the court, FCC lawyers assured the D.C. Circuit that, should NextWave prevail there, the company would be returned its licenses. Consequently, NextWave would suffer no irreparable harm if the auction were to proceed.

Perhaps based on this reassurance, the D.C. Circuit denied NextWave its petition for a stay. Both popular and industry press interpreted the court's decision as an indication that NextWave was unlikely to prevail. The FCC was determined to rush the NextWave licenses back to the auction block. Had the D.C. Circuit simply granted a stay at this juncture, the chaos surrounding events about to unfold could have been avoided. But there is no use blaming the court for failing to prevent the FCC from creating more problems for itself.

When Auction 35 finally took place, bidders could not be certain of the ultimate legal status of these licenses. They showed up, nonetheless, and bid more than $15 billion of real money for licenses that a few years earlier had fetched only a fraction of that amount in IOUs. But the cloud of litigation uncertainty hung over the auction. Like artworks of uncertain provenance, the spectrum license auction actually raised far less than it would have under circumstances of clear title. Practically all major wireless carriers participated, mostly through sponsored designated entities.

The FCC made specific statements that the auction was conditional on its success in the D.C. Circuit. While practically everyone associated with Auction 35 publicly proclaimed NextWave dead, few could avoid following the NextWave legal proceedings with some apprehension. The political value of holding the re-auction could not be underestimated. Having dozens of Auction 35 winners whose investment of time and money would become worthless if NextWave were to prevail provided the FCC with a stable of deep-pocketed and influential allies in its court case against NextWave. Rather than a lonely fight against industry, the FCC now found itself reinforced and resupplied with supporting briefs for the court and supporting calls to Capitol Hill, describing the value of the FCC's case to important constituents.

But the decisions of courts usually rest less with the number of friendly briefs than with the strength of their legal arguments. Industry observers were nervous after seeing the initial round of NextWave briefs in the fall of 2000, and positively frightened after oral arguments before the D.C. Circuit in the spring of 2001. NextWave was represented by, among others, Ted Olson, later solicitor general and top Supreme Court lawyer for the Bush administration, who launched a devastating attack on the FCC position. At oral arguments, the D.C. Circuit panel seemed skeptical of the FCC's position.

The court would not issue an opinion for a few more months, but the FCC had done so poorly that the Auction 35 winners began asking the commission to delay issuing their licenses. They did not want to be out-of-pocket pay for licenses that stood a good chance of being returned to NextWave. In the spring of 2001, everyone knew that FCC had done poorly in court, but no one knew just how poorly.

The D.C. Circuit Court Opinion

In June 2001, the D.C. Circuit Court issued one of its most devastating opinions against the FCC, strong even by the standards of a court that almost routinely ruled against the commission.[13] NextWave had raised several legal objections to the FCC's seizure of its licenses. The court went to extraordinary lengths to emphasize that it was sufficient to find for NextWave based only on its claim of the sanctity of bankruptcy law. It ordered a return of the licenses to NextWave and left aside for the time being a review of NextWave's other claims. Whether or not licenses could be forfeited or revoked was not even addressed. The court was especially careful to explain why its opinion did not conflict with the Second Circuit's opinion, in an effort to avoid a circuit court split, which could have prompted a Supreme Court review.

The D.C. Circuit Court decision was a crushing blow to the FCC and everyone who had joined the bandwagon to grab the NextWave licenses. Not only had the FCC lost in court again, but the path of appeal from there seemed impossibly difficult. To win would require first getting the Supreme Court to review the case and then have it find favorably for the FCC. After clearing those two very difficult hurdles, the FCC would face yet another round of litigation on NextWave's other unresolved legal issues before the same D.C. Circuit Court that seemed profoundly skeptical of anything the commission brought before it. The path to victory in litigation could take years and would require the FCC to prevail in each and every decision.

In the summer of 2001, after the D.C. Circuit Court decision, a delegation from NextWave met with high-ranking FCC officials to discuss the reinstatement of their licenses. NextWave had won in court and assumed this was simply a matter of timing, and the sooner the better. The delegation was informed that NextWave could get its licenses back soon, but threatened that the company might not be able to hold onto them for very long. First, the FCC could appeal the D.C. Circuit opinion to the Supreme Court. Second, the FCC had enormous discretion in interpreting rules and could easily find a regulatory basis for finding NextWave out of compliance with its rules as licensee—for example, on failing to build out service in a timely manner—if the FCC so chose. It was as if the court decision did not happen; the FCC could use its combination of governmental powers to work its will, with or without court approval.

Welcome to the Sausage Factory

On the other hand, NextWave could keep its licenses unmolested for a time if it agreed to participate with the FCC in a grand scheme whereby the Auction 35 winners would pay their winning bids, and the federal government and NextWave would split the receipts. It was a win-win strategy. The Auction 35 winners would get the spectrum they wanted at prices they were willing to pay, presumably less than they would have had to pay in an auction free of legal uncertainty. NextWave would get some value out of the deal, perhaps more than it could recoup from the decade of litigation against a taxpayer-funded army of lawyers. The FCC would recover some money for the government, too, although nothing close to what it would have realized had it run the auction properly from the start.

The government had substantial leverage over the Auction 35 winners, holding their more than $3 billion in down payments hostage and having a court appeal deadline serving as an effective negotiations deadline. All would be lost if the various parties didn't agree to last-minute concessions before the window closed on the FCC's own deadline for appealing to the Supreme Court for reversal of the D.C. Circuit Court's ruling. The details of this scheme of unknown sponsorship took months to negotiate and were not revealed until the Thanksgiving recess of 2001. They were negotiated among the administration, the FCC, the largest of the Auction 35 winners (smaller winners were purposefully and perhaps unlawfully excluded), and NextWave, away from public scrutiny and outside of any recognizable form of administrative law.

The scheme ultimately failed, not because the private parties could not reach an agreement with the administration and the FCC, but because the agreement they reached required Congress write a new law to accommodate it. Congress refused to rubberstamp the agreement. Ironically, had the private parties negotiated without government involvement, it is entirely possible that they could have reached an agreement that did not require new legislation. Conceivably, they could have reached similar financial terms for simple transfers of licenses, and the FCC could have conditioned the transfers on some compensation to the government. None of this would have required action by Congress.

The Market Collapses Again

After the deal fell apart at the end of 2001, most observers believed that NextWave would emerge from bankruptcy and sell its assets to any one of a number of interested buyers. Instead, in early 2002, the Supreme Court agreed to review the D.C. Circuit Court opinion. NextWave remained in bankruptcy. Perhaps the Supreme Court's decision to review the D.C. Circuit opinion meant that it was wrong all along. Perhaps it meant that communications law did trump bankruptcy law, and NextWave would join countless other telecommunications firms that had been crushed in recent years. All of this remained for the Supreme Court to disentangle.

In the meantime, the market values of wireless companies plummeted in 2002. Companies eager to participate in the deal at the end of 2001 became eager to avoid the same deal a few months later. The pendulum had swung once again, and spectrum prices that had seemed a bargain in Auction 35 in early 2001 seemed much too dear in 2002. The FCC had one last card to play: It held the Auction 35 winners accountable for their bids in the event that it prevailed in the Supreme Court. Not until late 2002 did the commission relieve the Auction 35 participants of their entangled obligations.[14] The decision to do so came only after all observers realized, following Supreme Court oral arguments, that the FCC would lose its case.

The actual Supreme Court opinion released in late January 2003 was somewhat anticlimactic.[15] No one who witnessed the oral arguments on October 8, 2002, had any doubt that the FCC would lose; the only issues were the number of dissents (one) and the extent of the defeat (complete and utter). Needless to say, the FCC issued no apologies.

For more than four years after entering bankruptcy court, NextWave had been confronted with a variety of FCC legal positions, each changing with the market and in response to the FCC's own strategic errors. The FCC used a series of adjudicatory positions, rulemakings, and enforcement postures in an attempt to remedy its serial errors. The tragedy is not just the fate of NextWave or any of the other parties involved. Practically every entity that was a part of the NextWave saga—competitors, courts, the FCC, and Congress—emerged the worse for it. At every turn, the FCC invented a new plan that employed one of its combined powers to extricate itself from its preceding mistake. In each instance, it turned a bad situation into

144 A TOUGH ACT TO FOLLOW?

something worse. If the powers of the FCC were divided among different agencies, each with but one of the powers of government, the NextWave saga could never have happened. The FCC would never have had the power to put itself in the predicament in which it ended up, and the public would be the richer for it.

The combined powers of government that the FCC exercised in the NextWave saga were largely residual from the Communications Act of 1934. The entire NextWave litigation happened after the passage of the Telecommunications Act of 1996. If the purpose of the Act were even partly to remedy the problems of the 1934 Act and to enhance competition and deregulation, NextWave demonstrates that the Act did not fully succeed.

Conclusion

The Telecommunications Act of 1996 was born with great hope. Congress only infrequently rewrites a law, and when it does so it is not because the law is working well, but precisely because it is not. Between the early 1970s and 1996, members of Congress broadly agreed that the Communications Act of 1934 was not working well.

It was variously thought that with the passage of a new law the problems that beset the antiquated Communications Act of 1934 would disappear; that new technologies would emerge; that competition would flourish; and that regulation as an important influence on the communications sector would recede.

But something went wrong. While communications regulation has changed much since the passage of the Act, it is difficult to find a direct and predictable correspondence between the Act and those changes. The FCC's implementation of the Telecommunications Act of 1996 has fallen far short of its potential. The Act has been tough to follow. On that single conclusion, there is little disagreement.

As to how to rectify this situation, there is little agreement. Some observers suggest the FCC needs more resources and staff to better implement the law. Yet the budget of the FCC has increased substantially since the passage of the Act, to no avail.

Another common suggestion is that the FCC would perform better if the Act were rewritten to incorporate different policies. Some in Congress believe that the problems with the Act lie in its wording, and that poor drafting in 1996 might be easily remedied now with a recasting of legislation. There is little evidence, however, that the problems that beset the FCC in recent years would be fully remedied with wordsmithing.

Even more unrealistic is the view that the 1996 Act has been overtaken by new technology. Unless one is willing to believe that technological change is unique to the period 1996–2005, the obsolescence explanation holds that Congress is condemned to rewrite communications law every few years to account for the latest developments. Yet in other areas of rapid technological change—intellectual property, pharmaceuticals, and bioscience, for example—laws change infrequently.

Also untenable is the suggestion that the FCC needs different leadership. The staff is honest, dedicated, and professional. Four different chairmen and more than a dozen different commissioners have presided over the FCC since the passage of the Act. They have all tried mightily to implement the Act lawfully and fairly. They have tried different regulatory approaches. But no chairman can change the law that combines the powers of government in the FCC.

The reason the Telecommunications Act of 1996 was not implemented precisely is the same reason that the Communications Act of 1934 was not implemented precisely: the combination of powers at the FCC makes it an unlikely institution to implement any statute precisely. The combination of powers places the commissioners and staff of the FCC in the awkward position of having no one but themselves to review and to balance their decisions. Even the most virtuous of public servants could not perform the functions of government well under such conditions.

Results of the Natural Experiment

Before 1996, large parts of the Code of Federal Regulations pertaining to the communications sector, and many administrative and adjudicatory decisions at the FCC, had little direct statutory basis. Justifications for these decisions were based on elastic phrases in the Communications Act of 1934. The FCC deftly wielded substantial powers by combining all of the powers of government. Courts would occasionally overturn some aspect of an FCC decision, only to see it reinvented elsewhere.

The 1996 Act was written in part to harness the FCC's discretion and channel it in a new direction. It was a reassertion of congressional political control over communications policy decisions. Specific and detailed instructions were not invitations to the FCC to continue with unbridled discretion.

At the beginning of this book, it was suggested that the Act is a natural experiment to examine whether the combination of powers matters in a small, isolated agency. If the FCC closely followed the new law with precise rules and efficient, nondiscriminatory administration and adjudication, then separation of powers would not be necessary for its proper implementation. That has not been the outcome. Indeed, it appears that the FCC was sloppy in writing rules under the 1996 Act and unable to restrain regulatory uncertainty, and occasionally appeared to engage in regulatory discrimination. No branch of government has reliably disciplined the FCC to insist on better performance. The combination of powers has apparently mattered.

A Cautionary Tale

The story of the FCC since the passage of the Telecommunications Act of 1996 is a cautionary tale. For anyone familiar with the current communications regulatory environment, even a casual perusal of the Act reveals many unexplored worlds. Entire sections seem to have no concrete meaning in the current realm of communications regulation. Yet much of the actual regulation of the communications sector is filled with words, concepts, and procedures alien to the Act.

The Act has not been followed, but not for want of trying. Every year, the FCC assigns hundreds of lawyers to do nothing but implement it. But the FCC has responsibilities and political interests taken from all of the branches of government. The interpretations of statute the FCC adopts in rulemaking are sloppy and sometimes bear little resemblance to the statute. The fear that regulated entities have of FCC retribution prevents all but a few instances of excess from ever facing a challenge in court.

The courts are painfully aware of the FCC's difficulty in following the Act. The commission is completely vindicated in fewer than half of the cases related to it. Court defeats are typically followed by months of denial and years of appeals, but rarely with a narrow effort to find a remedy. Many FCC court losses have not been fully resolved nearly a decade after passage of the Act.

Even more troubling is the residual effect of shoehorning the powers of the three branches of government into one agency. Shortcomings in rulemakings are compensated with adjustments in enforcement or adjudications, and vice versa. The incentive of a government official to write precise, legally defensible rules vanishes when that same official will later enforce or adjudicate the same rules. Officials who are asked to perform more than one of the three functions of government inevitably fall short in performing each of them. The shortcomings of agencies with the combined powers of government are not individual failures but institutional failures.

The loss is not merely the performance of governmental functions. As a result of the agency's stewardship over the sector, businesses regulated by the FCC have had greater rather than smaller costs of doing business, and more rather than less uncertainty about their legal rights. In response, they have rationally curtailed expansion plans, raised prices, lowered quality of service, developed an expertise in dealing with the FCC, or simply gone out of business. Consumers ultimately pay for this in higher prices for fewer services from fewer competitors.

Many laws are never properly or fully implemented, but the Telecommunications Act of 1996 is a particularly sobering example of failed implementation. Its story is one of both the limitless possibilities of improving the economic welfare of a nation by eliminating the rules that impede economic activity in the communications sector, and the consequences of falling short of those possibilities. The Act never came close to its potential.

When the government does a poor job of implementing its own laws, we are all the poorer. We lose both the economic security that graces a society in which laws are predictably and fairly enforced, and the reinforcement of democratic principles that comes from a successful effort to legislate, administer, and adjudicate by that rule of law. When a government agency may choose to treat parties unequally and treat some provisions of law as inconvenient suggestions, it is difficult to expect regulated private parties to maintain a respect for the laws that govern them.

Failure to Separate Powers

As illustrated in this book, the problems with the implementation of the Telecommunications Act of 1996 result in large part from the FCC's combination of powers. While it is tempting to prescribe a detailed separation-of-powers structure for the FCC, how that is ultimately accomplished matters less than accomplishing anything in that direction.

The FCC can muddle along forever with the combined powers of government, but one should not expect occasional changes in communications laws to have their specifically intended results. A problem that has festered for much of a century without adequate attention from Congress, the courts, or successive administrations is unlikely to be fixed without public demand for resolution. The remedy lies in changing the statutory structure of the FCC.

The many calls for rewriting the Act or for abandoning it altogether are a natural reaction by an industry in bad economic times that wants to change circumstances, including the law. But communications law has already been modified a few times since 1996, often with little effect.[1] Simply modifying or rewriting the specific policies in the Act may yield little benefit. A government agency that does a poor job of implementing one law isn't necessarily going to do a better job implementing the next iteration.

Few of the many commonly voiced arguments for rewriting the Act address separation of powers. Influential voices frequently call for statutory changes to benefit a particular industry or to advance a specific technology or policy, but they rarely address this fundamental flaw.

Many suggestions also focus on the *language* of the Act. One specific failing, most famously suggested by Justice Scalia, is that it is vague and ambiguous.[2] While certain language in certain sections is vague, most of the Act is unambiguous. Indeed, it is less ambiguous than the 1934 Act it replaced. Furthermore, vagueness in some sections of the Act does not constitute an invitation to the FCC to invent its own code.

This vagueness was not an accident, but rather a feature designed to gain passage of the Act, which more specific language might have jeopardized. Whole sections that are completely unambiguous have been left completely unimplemented. Moreover, vagueness in legislative language is not peculiar to the Act. The Act is arguably far more precise than many laws that have not raised Justice Scalia's ire. For all of the Act's infirmities and imprecision, both real and imagined, it is not obvious that there ever will be a broad majority in Congress to write communications law that is any less vaguely worded. Simply admonishing Congress do so avoids or ignores the critical flaw of the FCC's structure.

Nor does anything in recent jurisprudence suggest that the judicial branch will soon find fault with the combination of powers at the FCC. The courts have frequently addressed issues related to separation of powers, including delegation of legislative power, delegation of judicial power, presidential authority to remove officeholders, distinctions between rule-makings and adjudications, and procedural issues within the operations of administrative agencies. While they often reverse administrative agencies (although few, if any, are reversed as frequently as the FCC), these reversals do not establish a pattern that will inevitably lead to greater care for the separation of powers at such agencies.

In recent decades, private parties have rarely challenged the concentration of power of federal agencies. These parties perceive that the likelihood of success on the merits of the law is remote, that the likelihood of agency retaliation is too high, or both. Without a presentation of forceful arguments, courts will not by themselves find delegation of combined powers in government agencies unlawful or unconstitutional. Even when presented with such arguments, the courts themselves appear to go to extraordinary lengths to avoid a finding of concentration of power.[3]

The problems associated with the concentration of powers are not unique to the FCC. Other government agencies, such as the FDA, the SEC, and the EPA, have powers that should be divided among different agencies. The concentration of powers in some federal agencies dates back to the nineteenth century, making further inroads during the New Deal.[4] No administration since Franklin Roosevelt's has seriously attempted to bring all the functions of independent agencies into the executive branch, and that effort failed.[5]

How to Improve the Situation

The problem of concentration of powers in the FCC and other federal agencies is a reparable one. As de Tocqueville said, "The great privilege of the Americans is . . . not only to be more enlightened than others, but to have the ability to make reparable mistakes."[6]

But concern about the separation of powers in government agencies is not currently fashionable in political circles or even academic seminars. An eighteenth-century ideal that animated debate surrounding the adoption of the Constitution lies dormant today, as if the issue were no longer a concern. We confidently assume that we have inherited the benefits of the separation of powers, without ensuring that we still practice it.

Yet those inside the government agencies recognize that the combinations of powers do not work well. At the FCC itself, recent chairmen have been aware of the problems inherent in combined powers and have taken some steps to remedy them. Chairman Kennard established an enforcement bureau, mimicking the separate role of the executive branch. Many bureaus within the FCC have discrete rulemaking divisions.

Ultimately, however, internal organizational restructuring can take the separation of powers only so far. Different organizational units can be insulated from one another, but the principals to whom they are responsible cannot be disembodied from themselves.

The FCC is subject to a wide range of criticisms, from the sublime to the ridiculous, but its failure to separate governmental powers rarely, if ever, raises an eyebrow. In a democracy such as ours, laws do not change except through the consent, and insistence, of the governed. The Telecommunications Act of 1996 was poorly implemented because no one complained loudly and articulately about the harms from the FCC's combined powers. Communications regulation will improve only when those harmed by the FCC insist that it be repaired.

Appendix

FCC Merger Reviews
1997–2002

The FCC reviewed many mergers between 1997 and 2002. Tables A1 through A5 list some of the major mergers reviewed by the FCC by industry sector. The mergers included in the tables are primarily those listed at the merger review team Web site, with a few additions. The mergers listed are large, ranging in size from a few hundred million dollars to tens of billions of dollars.

The fourth column of tables A1 through A5 lists the number of days required to complete the review. The length of these delays ranges from 73 to 730 days. Of the forty-six mergers listed, only five took the ninety days or less to review, as directed by the Act.

Mergers involving foreign ownership review are also noted. They do not appear to have taken substantially more or less time for the FCC to process than other mergers.

TABLE A1

MERGERS REVIEWED BY THE FCC

LICENSE TRANSFER APPLICATIONS

PRIMARILY WIRELINE TELECOMMUNICATIONS

	Date applied	Date approved	Days delayed	Delegated authority	Ad hoc conditions[a]
WorldCom-MFS[b][1]	Sept.13, 1996	Dec. 5, 1996	83	Yes	[d]
SBC–Pacific Telesis[2]	June 7, 1996	Jan. 31, 1997	238	No	[d]
Bell Atlantic– NYNEX[3]	April 22, 1996[e]	Aug. 14, 1997	479	No	FCC
Qwest-LCI[b][4]	March 9, 1998[e]	May 21, 1998	73	Yes	[d]
AT&T-Teleport[5]	Feb. 3, 1998	July 21, 1998	168	No	[d]
WorldCom-MCI[6]	Oct. 1, 1997[f]	Sept. 14, 1998	348	No	FCC
SBC-SNET[7]	Feb. 20, 1998	Oct. 15, 1998	237	No	FCC
SBC-Ameritech[8]	July 24, 998	Oct. 6, 1999	439	No	FCC
AT&T–British Telecommuni- cations[9]	Nov. 10, 1998	Oct. 22, 1999	346	No	FCC, DOD, DOJ, FBI
Qwest–U.S. West[10]	Aug. 19, 1999	March 8, 2000	202	No	FCC
Bell Atlantic–GTE[11]	Oct. 2, 1998	June 16, 2000	624	No	FCC
Verizon-OnePoint[12]	Sept. 5, 2000	Dec. 8, 2000	94	Yes	[d]
WorldCom- Intermedia[13]	Oct. 10, 2000	Jan. 17, 2001	86	Yes	FCC condition on compliance with DOJ proceeding

(continued on next page)

(continued from previous page)

	Date applied	Date approved	Days delayed	Delegated authority	Ad hoc conditions[a]
Global Crossing–Frontier[14]	Oct. 10, 2000	April 16, 2001	188	Yes	d
TDS–Chorus Communications[15]	Feb. 8, 2001	Aug. 10, 2001	183	Yes	d
XO Communi- cations Reorgani- zation[c][16]	Feb. 21, 2002	Oct. 3, 2002	224	Yes	DOJ, FBI

NOTES:
a. Conditions beyond what is necessary to come into compliance with FCC rules.
b. Not listed at FCC merger review team Web site.
c. Foreign ownership review.
d. No conditions listed in order beyond what is necessary to come into compliance with FCC rules.
e. Announced.
f. Subsequently amended.

TABLE A2

MERGERS REVIEWED BY THE FCC LICENSE TRANSFER APPLICATIONS PRIMARILY CABLE ASSETS

	Date applied	Date approved	Days delayed	Delegated authority	Ad hoc conditions[a]
AT&T-TCI[17]	Sept. 14, 1998	Feb. 17, 1999	156	No	FCC
AT&T-MediaOne[18]	July 7, 1999	June 5, 2000	334	No	FCC
AOL–Time Warner[19]	Feb. 11, 2000	Jan. 11, 2001	335	No	FCC
Comcast-AT&T[20]	Feb. 28, 2002	Nov. 13, 2002	258	No	FCC

NOTE:
a. Conditions beyond what is necessary to come into compliance with FCC rules.

TABLE A3

MERGERS REVIEWED BY THE FCC LICENSE TRANSFER APPLICATIONS
PRIMARILY SATELLITE SERVICES

	Date applied	Date approved	Days delayed	Delegated authority	Ad hoc conditions[a]
Lockheed-Comsat[21]	Sept.15, 1999	July 27, 2000	316	No	[b]
SES Global–GE Americom[c 22]	April 2, 2001	Oct.1, 2001	183	Yes	[b]
Telenor Satellite–Comsat[c 23]	May 4, 2001	Dec. 14, 2001	224	No	FCC, DOJ, FBI
Iridium (New)–Iridium[c 24]	March 19, 2001	Feb. 8, 2002	326	Yes	DOJ, FBI
ORBCOMM–Orbital Communications Corp.[c 25]	July 25, 2001	March 8, 2002	226	Yes	[b]

NOTES:
a. Conditions beyond what is necessary to come into compliance with FCC rules.
b. No conditions listed in order beyond what is necessary to come into compliance with FCC rules.
c. Foreign ownership review.

TABLE A4

MERGERS REVIEWED BY THE FCC

LICENSE TRANSFER APPLICATIONS

PRIMARILY WIRELESS TELECOMMUNICATIONS

	Date applied	Date approved	Days delayed	Delegated authority	Ad Hoc Conditions[a]
Vodafone–AirTouch[b] [26]	Feb. 5, 1999	June 21, 1999	136	No	DOD, DOJ, FBI
SBC–Comcast Wireless[b] [27]	March 4, 1999	July 2, 1999	120	Yes	[c]
VoiceStream–Cook Inlet[d] [28]	July 15, 1999	Feb. 14, 2000	214	No	DOJ, FBI
Arch Communications–Paging Network[29]	Dec. 13, 1999	April 25, 2000	133	Yes	[c]
SBC–BellSouth–Cingular[30]	May 4, 2000	Sept. 29, 2000	148	Yes	[c]
TeleCorp, Tritel, and Indus PCS[31]	April 27, 2000	Oct. 27, 2000	183	Yes	[c]
VoiceStream–Cook Inlet[d] [32]	Sept. 25, 2000	Dec. 13, 2000	79	Yes	[c]
Verizon-ALLTEL[33]	Nov. 13, 2000	Feb. 28, 2001	107	Yes	[c]
Nextel-Motorola[34]	Sept. 25, 2000	April 16, 2001	203	Yes	[c]
Deutsche Telekom–VoiceStream[d] [35]	Sept. 18, 2000	April 24, 2001	218	No	DOJ, FBI
Nextel–Arch Wireless[36]	Feb. 16, 2001	May 25, 2001	98	Yes	[c]
Nextel–Pacific Wireless[37]	July 27, 2001	Nov. 16, 2001	112	Yes	[c]
Nextel-Chadmoore[38]	July 6, 2001	Nov. 30, 2001	147	Yes	[c]

(continued on next page)

(continued from previous page)

	Date applied	Date approved	Days delayed	Delegated authority	Ad hoc conditions[a]
AT&T Wireless–Telecorp PCS[39]	Oct. 24, 2001	Feb. 12, 2002	111	Yes	c
ALLTEL-CenturyTel[40]	March 28, 2002	June 12, 2002	76	Yes	c

NOTES:
a. Conditions beyond what is necessary to come into compliance with FCC rules.
b. Not listed at FCC merger review team Web site.
c. No conditions listed in order beyond what is necessary to come into compliance with FCC rules.
d. Foreign ownership review.

TABLE A5

MERGERS REVIEWED BY THE FCC
LICENSE TRANSFER APPLICATIONS
PRIMARILY BROADCASTING ASSETS

	Date applied	Date approved	Days delayed	Delegated authority	Ad hoc conditions[a]
Westinghouse-Infinity[b] [41]	June 20, 1996[c]	Dec. 26, 1996	189	No	FCC
Viacom-CBS[42]	Nov. 16, 1999	May 3, 2000	169	No	FCC
Clearchannel-AMFM[43]	Nov. 16, 1999	Aug. 7, 2000	265	No	FCC
Newscorp–Chris-Craft[44]	Sept. 8, 2000	July 23, 2001	318	No	a
Sinclair-Glencairn[b] [45]	Nov. 16, 1999	Nov. 15, 2001	730	No	FCC
NBC-Telemundo[46]	Nov. 1, 2001	April 9, 2002	160	No	FCC

NOTES:
a. Conditions beyond what is necessary to come into compliance with FCC rules.
b. Not listed at FCC merger review team Web site.
c. Announced.

Notes

Chapter 1: Separation of Powers and Dashed Expectations

1. Throughout the book, I use the term *communications sector* to refer broadly to those industries heavily regulated by the Federal Communications Commission, including telecommunications, broadcasting, cable, wireless communications, and satellite communications.

2. For a brief summary of these checks and balances, see *The U.S. Constitution Online*, "Constitutional Topics: Checks and Balances," http://www.usconstitution.net/consttop_cnb.html (accessed July 21, 2005), or *Wikipedia*, s.v. "Separation of Powers," http://en.wikipedia.org/wiki/Separation_of_powers#Checks_and_balances (accessed July 21, 2005).

3. See P. B. Kurland and R. Lerner, eds., *The Founders' Constitution*, chapter 10, http://press-pubs.uchicago.edu/founders (accessed August 21, 2005).

4. See, e.g., John Adams, "Thoughts on Government," *Collected Papers*, vol. 4, 86–93, http://press-pubs.uchicago.edu/founders/documents/v1ch4s5.html (accessed August 21, 2005).

5. *Myers v. United States*, 272 U.S. 52 (1926), notes.

6. See, e.g., *Federalist Papers* 9, 10, 47, 48, and 51.

7. Kurland and Lerner, *The Founders' Constitution*, chapter 10.

8. Other independent agencies at the federal level include the Federal Trade Commission, the Federal Energy Regulatory Commission, the Consumer Product Safety Commission, and the Nuclear Regulatory Commission, to name just a few.

9. In a dissent in *Federal Maritime Commission v. South Carolina State Ports Authority*, 535 U.S. 743 (2002), affirmed, Justice Breyer asserts that the constitutional status of independent agencies within the executive branch is settled law:

> At the outset one must understand the constitutional nature of the legal proceeding before us. The legal body conducting the proceeding, the Federal Maritime Commission, is an "independent" federal agency. Constitutionally speaking, an "independent" agency belongs neither to the Legislative Branch nor to the Judicial Branch of Government.

Although Members of this Court have referred to agencies as a "fourth branch" of Government, *FTC v. Ruberoid Co.*, 343 U.S. 470, 487 (1952) (Jackson, J., dissenting), the agencies, even "independent" agencies, are more appropriately considered to be part of the Executive Branch. See *Freytag v. Commissioner,* 501 U.S. 868, 910 (1991) (Scalia, J., concurring in part and concurring in judgment). The President appoints their chief administrators, typically a Chairman and Commissioners, subject to confirmation by the Senate. Cf. *Bowsher v. Synar,* 478 U.S. 714, 723 (1986). The agencies derive their legal powers from congressionally enacted statutes. And the agencies enforce those statutes, *i.e.,* they "execute" them, in part by making rules or by adjudicating matters in dispute. Cf. *Panama Refining Co. v. Ryan,* 293 U.S. 388, 428–29 (1935).

The Court long ago laid to rest any constitutional doubts about whether the Constitution permitted Congress to delegate rulemaking and adjudicative powers to agencies. *E.g., ICC v. Cincinnati, N. O. & T. P. R. Co.,* 167 U.S. 479, 494–95 (1897) (permitting rulemaking); *Crowell v. Benson,* 285 U.S. 22, 46 (1932) (permitting adjudication); *Commodity Futures Trading Comm'n v. Schor,* 478 U.S. 833, 852 (1986) (same). That, in part, is because the Court established certain safeguards surrounding the exercise of these powers. See, *e.g., A. L. A. Schechter Poultry Corp. v. United States,* 295 U.S. 495 (1935) (nondelegation doctrine); *Crowell,* supra (requiring judicial review). And the Court denied that those activities as safeguarded, however much they might *resemble* the activities of a legislature or court, fell within the scope of Article I or Article III of the Constitution. *Schechter Poultry,* supra, at 529–30; *Crowell,* supra, at 50–53; see also *INS v. Chadha,* 462 U.S. 919, 953, n. 16 (1983) (agency's use of rulemaking "resemble[s]," but is not, lawmaking). Consequently, in exercising those powers, the agency is engaging in an Article II, Executive Branch activity. And the powers it is exercising are powers that the Executive Branch of Government must possess if it is to enforce modern law through administration.

10. For a review of judicial expansion of congressional delegation, particularly with respect to independent agencies, see "Annotations of Article I of the Constitution: Delegation of Legislative Power," http://supreme.lp.findlaw.com/constitution/article01/04.html, (accessed August 21, 2005).

Chapter 2: The Ancestry of the FCC

1. In most legal systems, there are different tiers for the writing of laws, the administration of those laws, and the resolution of disputes under those laws.

Under federal law are at least three different levels: (1) the actual statutes that comprise the U.S. Code; (2) the rules implementing these statutes, promulgated subject to the Administrative Procedures Act and codified in the Code of Federal Rules (CFR); and (3) the precedents, opinion letters, and administrative interpretations made by agencies that implement the CFR. In each tier, binding law is made, the law is administered, and disputes are resolved. One of the most salient features of this administrative law is that government agencies do not have unlimited powers, and the rules they promulgate must be authorized by a higher level of law. Thus, letters or memoranda written by an agency should refer to rules in the CFR, which in turn should refer to statutes.

2. 47 U.S.C. 207.

3. 47 U.S.C. 4(i).

4. 47 U.S.C. 201.

5. 47 U.S.C. 303.

6. See, e.g., *FCC v. Pottsville Broadcasting Co.*, 309 U.S. 134 (1940).

7. Ibid.

8. See Steve Coll, *The Deal of the Century: The Breakup of AT&T* (New York: Atheneum, 1986), 92–100.

9. See P. W. Huber, M. K. Kellogg, and J. Thorne, *Federal Telecommunications Law*, 2d ed. (Gaithersburg: Aspen Law & Business, 2000), chapter 1, for part of this history.

10. Modification of Final Judgment, reprinted in *United States v. American Tel. & Tel. Co.*, 552 F. Supp. 131, 225–34 (D.D.C. 1982), aff'd sub nom. *Maryland v. United States*, 460 U.S. 1001 (1983).

11. See Huber, Kellogg, and Thorne, *Federal Telecommunications Law*, 44–46.

12. S. M. Besen, "AM versus FM: The Battle of the Bands," *Industrial and Corporate Change* 1, no. 2 (1992), 375–96.

13. See R. W. Crandall and H. W. Furchtgott-Roth, *Cable TV: Regulation or Competition?* (Washington, D.C.: Brookings Institution, 1996). See also T. W. Hazlett and M. L. Spitzer, *Public Policy Toward Cable Television* (Cambridge, Mass.: MIT Press, and Washington, D.C.: AEI Press, 1997).

14. J. H. Rohlfs, C. L. Jackson, and T. E. Kelly, "Estimate of the Loss to the United States Caused by the FCC's Delay in Licensing Cellular Telecommunications," paper prepared for National Economic Research Associates, White Plains, New York, November 8, 1991 (revised); and J. Hausman, "Valuing The Effect Of Regulation On New Services in Telecommunications," in *Brookings Papers on Economic Activity, Microeconomics, 1997*, eds. M. N. Bailey, P. C. Reiss, and C. Winston (Washington, D.C.: Brookings Press, 1997), 1–37.

15. Sec. 7a, *Clayton Act*, 15 U.S.C. 18a.

16. Time Warner Entertainment Co., L.P. v. FCC, http://www.fcc.gov/ogc/documents/opinions/2001/94-1035.html, 240 F.3d 1126 (D.C. Cir. 2001).

17. See *Red Lion Broadcasting Co. v. FCC*, 395 U.S. 367 (1969).

18. House Committee on Commerce, *Survey of Federal Agencies on Costs of Federal Regulations*, 105th Cong., 1st sess., H. Rep. 97-272-1, January 1997.

19. For some of the advantages of rational regulation associated with accounting for the costs of regulation, see R. Hahn, *Reviving Regulatory Reform: A Global Perspective* (Washington, D.C.: AEI Press, 2000).

20. H. Furchtgott-Roth (commissioner), *Report on the Implementation of Section 11 by the Federal Communications Commission*, prepared for the Federal Communications Commission, December 21, 1998.

21. For an example of the evolution of the interpretation of rules, see J. G. Sidak, *Foreign Investment in American Telecommunications* (Chicago, Ill.: University of Chicago Press, 1997).

22. *Cable Act of 1992*, 102d Cong., 2d sess., H.R.4850, *Congressional Record* 138 (September 17, 1992): H8687; *Cable Act of 1992*, 102d Cong., 2d sess., S.12, *Congressional Record* 138 (September 22, 1992): S14616.

23. *Congressional Record* 138 (House, October 5, 1992): H11488, and (Senate, October 5, 1992): S16676.

24. Crandall and Furchtgott-Roth, *Cable TV: Regulation or Competition?* 40–43.

25. Ibid., 81–83.

Chapter 3: The Telecommunications Act of 1996

1. *AT&T v. Iowa Utilities Board,* 525 U.S. 366 (1999).

2. R. Hundt, *You Say You Want a Revolution* (New Haven, Conn.: Yale University Press, 2000).

3. See NASDAQ Telecommunications Index, 1996–2000, Series ^IXUT, http://finance.yahoo.com/q/hp?s=%5EIXUT (accessed August 21, 2005).

4. Ibid.

5. The exact magnitude of the stock market loss depends on the boundaries of the communications sector. Even a narrow market definition of the communications sector leads to market capitalization losses well in excess of one trillion dollars. For various assessments of the size of the loss, see, e.g., Mary Meeker and the Technology Team, *The Technology IPO Yearbook*, 8th ed. (N.Y.: Morgan Stanley, 2002); R. Litan, *The Telecommunications Crash: What to Do Now?* Policy Brief 112, Brookings Institution, December 2002; B. Hozemer, "The Telecom Bubble Has Burst, Now What?" August 2002, http://telecomassets.com/TAM_whitepaper.pdf (accessed August 21, 2005); and Kevin Maney, "Future Not So Bright for Telecoms," *USA Today*, July 15, 2002.

6. See Department of Commerce data on contribution of industries to Gross Domestic Product: http://www.bea.gov/bea/pn/GDPbyInd_VA_SIC.xls; http://www.bea.gov/bea/pn/GDPbyInd_GO_SIC.xls; http://www.bea.gov/bea/pn/GDPbyInd_GO_NAICS.xls (accessed August 21, 2005).

7. For a review of stock market bubbles, see K. Hassett, *Bubbleology* (New York: Crown Business, 2002).

Chapter 4: The Courts and the Administration
Will Not Discipline the FCC

1. *Federal Radio Comm. v. Nelson Bros. Bond & Mortgage Co.*, 289 U.S. 266 (1933), and *National Broadcasting Co. v. United States*, 319 U.S. 190 (1943).

2. *United States v. Southwestern Cable Co.*, 392 U.S. 157 (1968), granting power to regulate cable television under the Communications Act of 1934.

3. *Red Lion Broadcasting Co. v. FCC*, 395 U.S. 367 (1969).

4. *FCC v. RCA Communications*, 346 U.S. 86 (1953).

5. *FCC v. Pottsville Broadcasting Co.*

6. *AT&T v. Iowa Utilities Board.*

7. Ibid., 29–30.

8. The relevant language on which the Supreme Court's opinion in *Iowa Utilities Board* seems to hinge is, "The Commission may prescribe such rules and regulations as may be *necessary* in the public interest to carry out the provisions of this Act" [emphasis added]. 47 U.S.C. section 201(b).

9. "Except as provided in sections 223 through 227, inclusive, and section 332, and subject to the provisions of section 301 and title VI, nothing in this Act shall be construed to apply or to give the Commission jurisdiction with respect to (1) charges, classifications, practices, services, facilities, or regulations for or in connection with intrastate communication service by wire or radio of any carrier…," 47 U.S.C. section 2(b).

10. 47 U.S.C., sec. 152 and 201.

11. H.R. 1555, 104th Congress, sec. 101.

12. But even the discretion of the FCC had limits. The Court said that the FCC had to clearly and rationally explain its decisions, thus requiring those decisions to meet some minimal standard of exposition and rationality. See, for example, the discussion of unbundled network elements in *Iowa Utilities Board*.

13. *Chevron U.S.A., Inc. v. Natural Resources Defense Council, Inc.*, 467 U.S. 837 (1984).

14. Ibid., 842–43.

15. As stated in *Natl. Pub. Radio, Inc. v. FCC*, 349 U.S. App. D.C. 149, 254, F.3d 226 (2001).

16. *Chevron U.S.A., Inc. v. Natural Resources Defense Council, Inc.*, 865.

17. Ibid.

18. Ibid., 865–66.

19. See *Texas Office of Public Utility Counsel et al. v. FCC*, 183 F.3d 393 (5th Cir. 1999).

20. Frank Ahrens, "FCC Ordered to Review TV-Station Ownership Rules," *Washington Post*, April 3, 2002.

21. Consider, for example, FCC rules on political advertising and FTC rules on commercial advertising.

22. See FCC 00-360, *In the Matter of Repeal or Modification of the Personal Attack and Political Editorial Rules, MM Docket No. 83-484,* separate dissenting statements of M. K. Powell and H. Furchtgott-Roth, October 10, 2000.

23. FCC 99-393, *In Re Applications of WQED Pittsburgh and Cornerstone Television, Inc. (file number BALET-970602IA), et al.*, separate statements of commissioners Powell and Furchtgott-Roth approving in part and dissenting in part, December 29, 1999.

24. See FCC 99-72, *First Report and Order and Further Notice of Proposed Rulemaking, Truth-in-Billing and Billing Format; (CC Docket 98-17),* dissenting statement of H. Furchtgott-Roth, May 11, 1999.

25. Ibid.

26. *Radio-Television News Directors Association and National Association of Broadcasters v. FCC*, D.C. Circuit Court, 98-1305, filed October 11, 2000.

27. *USTA v. FCC*, 290 F.3d 415. (DC Cir. 2002),

28. There were 2,817 such documents on October 22, 2002.

29. 47 U.S.C., section 254.

30. See e.g., FCC 01-131, *Re: Implementation of the Local Competition Provisions in the Telecommunications Act of 1996 and Inter-Carrier Compensation for ISP-Bound Traffic, Order on Remand and Report and Order, CC Docket Nos. 96-98, 99-68,* dissenting statement of Commissioner H. Furchtgott-Roth, April 27, 2001.

31. *Telecommunications Act of 1996*, Public Law 104-104, *U.S. Statutes at Large* 110 (1996): 56, section 202.

32. 47 U.S.C., section 161.

33. For example, rules for portions of 47 U.S.C. 251, 252, and 254 have either never been written, never withstood court scrutiny, or constantly changed.

34. *Telecommunications Act of 1996*, section 202. This section requires the FCC to review its media ownership rules in each even-numbered year from 1998 onward.

35. See FCC 00-191, *1998 Biennial Regulatory Review*, adopted May 26, 2000, released June 20, 2000.

Chapter 5: Congress Will Not Discipline the FCC

1. *FCC v. Pottsville Broadcasting Co.*

2. 47 U.S.C. 254(h)(1)(b).

3. See House Ways and Means Committee, Subcommittee on Oversight, "Funding Mechanisms of the E-Rate Program," 105th Cong., 2d sess., Serial No. 105-108, statement of H. Furchtgott-Roth, August 4, 1998; J. Hausman, *Taxation by Telecommunications Regulation: The Economics of the E-Rate* (Washington, D.C.: AEI Press, 1998).

4. Fifth Circuit Court, *Texas Office of Public Utility Counsel et al. v. FCC*, no. 97-60421, decision issued July 30, 1999.

5. See House Ways and Means Committee, Subcommittee on Oversight, "Funding Mechanisms of the E-Rate Program."

6. Hamilton, *Federalist 15*.

7. Ibid.

8. *Texas Office of Public Utility Counsel et al. v. FCC*, 183 F.3d 393 (5th Cir. 1999).

9. Hausman, *Taxation by Telecommunications Regulation*.

10. See House Ways and Means Committee, Subcommittee on Oversight, "Funding Mechanisms of the E-Rate Program."

11. U.S. General Accounting Office, "Comments on the Federal Communications Commission's Implementation of Section 254," B-278820, letter from Robert P. Murphy, general counsel, to Senator Ted Stevens, February 10, 1998.

12. See, e.g., Senate Committee on Commerce, Science, and Transportation, "FCC Reauthorization Hearing," 105th Cong., 2d sess., S. Hearing 105-1042, opening statement of Senator John McCain, June 10, 1998.

13. *Texas Office of Public Utility Counsel et al. v. FCC*, 183 F.3d 393 (5th Cir. 1999).

Chapter 6: Individuals Do Not or Cannot Discipline the FCC

1. For a good introduction to the political economy of regulation and deregulation, see R. G. Noll and B. M. Owen, eds., *The Political Economy of Deregulation: Interest Groups in the Regulatory Process* (Washington, D.C.: AEI Press, 1983). Also, see R. G. Noll, *The Economics and Politics of the Slowdown in Regulatory Reform* (Washington, D.C.: AEI-Brookings Joint Center for Regulatory Studies, 1999).

2. See Harold Furchtgott-Roth (FCC commissioner) to Rep. George W. Gekas (chairman, House Judiciary Subcommittee on Commercial and Administrative Law), memorandum regarding impact of *American Trucking Ass'n v. EPA* on FCC rulemaking under section 254 of the Telecommunications Act of 1996, September 16, 1999.

3. Hundt, *You Say You Want a Revolution*.

4. 47 U.S.C., section 254.

5. FCC 97-411, *Universal Service, Third Order on Reconsideration*, dissenting statement of H. Furchtgott-Roth, December 16, 1997.

6. H. Furchtgott-Roth, "Volunteerism and the FCC," (speech before the Media Institute, Washington, D.C., November 17, 1998).

7. See, e.g., FCC 99-279, *Applications of Ameritech Corp. (Transferor) and SBC Communications, Inc. (Transferee), for Consent to Transfer Control of Corporations Holding Commission Licenses and Lines Pursuant to Sections 214 and 310(d) of the Communications Act and Parts 5, 22, 24, 25, 63, 90, 95, and 101 of the Commission's Rules, CC Docket 98-141*, statement of H. Furchtgott-Roth, concurring in part and dissenting in part, October 6, 1999.

8. *Association of Communications Enterprises v. FCC*, D.C. Circuit Docket No. 99-1441, decided January 9, 2001. See also FCC, "Furchtgott-Roth Reacts to D.C. Circuit Court Decision Vacating SBC-Ameritech Merger," press release, January 10, 2001.

9. *Texas Office of Public Utility Counsel et al. v. FCC*, Fifth Circuit Court, No. 97-60421, decision issued July 30, 1999.

Chapter 7: Sloppy Rulemaking

1. *United States Telecom Association v. FCC*, U.S. App. D.C. (No. 00-1012) (2004).

2. The usual citations include 47 U.S.C., sections 1, 4(i), 201, and 301.

3. FCC 00-258, *Implementation of Video Description of Video Programming*, MM Docket 99-339, August 7, 2000.

4. Ibid., separate statements of Commissioners Furchtgott-Roth and Powell.

5. *Motion Picture Association of America, Inc., et al. v. FCC*, 309 F.3d 796 (D.C. Cir. 2002) [No. 01-1149, November 8, 2002].

6. Ibid.

7. See, e.g., FCC 03-9, *In the Matter of Telecommunications Services Inside Wiring; Customer Premises Equipment; In the Matter of the Implementation of the Cable Television Consumer Protection and Competition Act of 1992; Cable Home Wiring; First Order on Reconsideration and Second Report and Order*, adopted January 21, 2002. See in particular dissent of Commissioner Kevin Martin.

8. Ray claims to be the original author of all of Billy Tauzin's "Boudreau" jokes.

9. House Ways and Means Committee, Subcommittee on Oversight, "Funding Mechanisms of the E-Rate Program."

10. *Grid Radio v. FCC*, 349 U.S. App. D.C. 365, 278 F.3d 1314 (2002); *Fox Television Stations, Inc. v. FCC*, 280 F.3d 1027 (D.C. Cir. 2002).

11. See, e.g., *AT&T v. Iowa Utilities Board*.

12. For example, after the Supreme Court issued its opinion in *AT&T v. Iowa Utilities Board*, many different parties claimed victory.

13. Missing from the sample, for example, are the district court and bankruptcy court opinions for GWI and NextWave, discussed in chapter 10.

14. See, e.g., *Goldwasser v. Ameritech*, 222 F.3d 390 (7th Cir. 2000); *Verizon Communications, Inc. v. Law Offices of Curtis V. Trinko, L.L.P.*, 124 S. Ct. 8782 (2004).

15. House Committee on Commerce, *Survey of Federal Agencies on Costs of Federal Regulations*.

16. See H. Furchtgott-Roth, *Report on Implementation of Section 11*.

17. Ibid.

18. Public Law 106-113, Section 213, November 29, 1999.

19. FCC, Wireless Bureau, DA 00-941, Public Notice, "Auction of Licenses for the 700 MHz Bands Postponed until September 6, 2000," and FCC, DA 00-942, Public Notice, May 2, 2000.

Chapter 8: Unpredictable FCC Rules and Communications Law

1. See FCC 99-404, *In the Matter of Application by Verizon Under Section 271 of the Telecommunications Act of 1996 To Provide In-Region, InterLATA Services in New York*, December 21, 1999, concurring statement of Commissioner Harold W. Furchtgott-Roth; FCC 00-238, *In the Matter of Application by SBC Communications Inc., Southwestern Bell Telephone Company, and Southwestern Bell Communications Services, Inc. d/b/a Southwestern Bell Long Distance Pursuant to Section 271 of the Telecommunications Act of 1996 To Provide In-Region, InterLATA Services in Texas*, concurring statement of Commissioner Harold W. Furchtgott-Roth, June 30, 2000; see also FCC 01-29, *In the Matter of Application by SBC Communications Inc., Southwestern Bell Telephone Company, and Southwestern Bell Communications Services, Inc. d/b/a Southwestern Bell Long Distance Pursuant to Section 271 of the Telecommunications Act of 1996 To Provide In-Region, InterLATA Services in Kansas and Oklahoma, CC Docket 00-217*, concurring statement of Commissioner Harold W. Furchtgott-Roth, January 22, 2001.

2. FCC 96-325, *Implementation of the Local Competition Provisions in the Telecommunications Act of 1996*, First Report and Order, August 8, 1996.

3. *Bell Atlantic Telephone Cos. v. FCC*, 206 F.3d 1 (D.C. Cir. 2000).

4. FCC 99-38, *In the Matter of Implementation of the Local Competition Provisions in the Telecommunications Act of 1996, CC Docket No. 96-98; ISP-Bound Provisions in the Telecommunications Act of 1996, Inter-Carrier Compensation for ISP-Bound Traffic, CC Docket No. 99-68; Declaratory Ruling in CC Docket No. 96-98 and Notice of Proposed Rulemaking in CC Docket No. 99-68*, February 25, 1999. See also FCC 01-131, *In the Matter of Developing a Unified Intercarrier Compensation Regime, CC Docket 01-92, NPRM*, April 19, 2001.

5. *WorldCom, Inc. v. FCC*, 246 F.3d 690 (D.C. Cir. 2001) [No. 00-1002, April 20, 2001]; *Global NAPs, Inc. v. FCC*, 247 F.3d 252 (D.C. Cir. 2001) [No. 00-1136, April 27, 2001]; and *WorldCom, Inc. v. FCC*, 288 F.3d 429(D.C. Cir. 2002). [No. 01-1218, May 3, 2002].

6. FCC 96-325, *Implementation of the Local Competition Provisions in the Telecommunications Act of 1996*, First Report and Order, August 8, 1996.

7. *AT&T Corp. v. Iowa Utilities Board*, 119 S. Ct. 721, 142 L.Ed.2d 835 (1999).

8. *Iowa Utilities Board v. FCC*, 120 F.3d 753 (8th Cir. 1997) and *Southwestern Bell Telephone Co. v. FCC*, 153 F.3d 597 (8th Cir. 1998) [No. 97-3389, August 10, 1998].

9. *Southwestern Bell Telephone Company et al. v. FCC*, 199 F.3d 996 (8th Cir. 1999) [No. 97-3389, December 27, 1999.] and *United States Telecom Association et al. v. FCC*, 290 F.3d 415 (D.C. Cir. 2002)

10. FCC 96-325, *Implementation of the Local Competition Provisions*.

11. *GTE Service Corp. v. FCC*, 205 F.3d 416 (D.C. Cir 2000).

12. *Verizon Telephone Companies et al. v. FCC*, 292 F.3d 903 (D.C. Cir. 2002)

13. FCC 99-355, *In the Matters of Deployment of Wireline Services Offering Advanced Telecommunications Capability and Implementation of the Local Competition Provisions of the Telecommunications Act of 1996, Third Report and Order in CC Docket*

No. 98-147 and Fourth Report and Order in CC Docket No. 96-98, November 18, 1999, 14 FCC Rcd 20912 (1999).

14. *United States Telecom Association et al. v. FCC*, 290 F.3d 415 (D.C. Cir. 2002).

15. FCC 96-325, *Implementation of the Local Competition Provisions*.

16. *Iowa Utilities Board v. FCC*, 120 F.3d 753 (8th Cir. 1997).

17. *Verizon Communications, Inc. v. FCC*, 535 U.S. 467, 122 S. Ct. 1646, 152 L.Ed.2d 701 (2002).

18. *AT&T Corp. v. Iowa Utilities Board*, 119 S. Ct. 721, 142 L.Ed.2d 835 (1999), and *Iowa Utilities Board v. FCC*, 219 F.3d 744 (8th Cir. 2000) [Nos. 96-3321, July 18, 2000].

19. FCC 98-027, *Telecommunications Carriers' Use of Customer Proprietary Network Information and Other Customer Information, Second Report and Order and Further Notice of Proposed Rulemaking*, CC Docket 96-149, February 19, 1998.

20. *U.S. West, Inc. v. FCC*, 182 F.3d 1224 (10th Cir. 1999) [No. 98-9518, August 18, 1999].

21. FCC 02-214, *Telecommunications Carriers' Use of Customer Proprietary Network Information and Other Customer Information; Implementation of the Non-Accounting Safeguards of Sections 271 and 272 of the Communications Act of 1934, as Amended 2000 Biennial Regulatory Review—Review of Policies and Rules Concerning Unauthorized Changes of Consumers' Long Distance Carriers*, CC Docket No. 96-115, CC Docket No. 96-149, CC Docket No. 00- 257, Third Report and Order and Third Further Notice of Proposed Rulemaking, adopted July 16, 2002, released July 25, 2002.

22. FCC 01-29, *In the Matter of Joint Application by SBC Communications Inc., Southwestern Bell Telephone Company, and Southwestern Bell Communications Services, Inc. d/ b/ a Southwestern Bell Long Distance for Provision of In-Region, InterLATA Services in Kansas and Oklahoma*, January 22, 2001.

23. *Sprint Communications Company, L.P. v. FCC*, 348 U.S. App. D.C., 266, 274 F.3d 549 (2001).

24. *WorldCom, Inc. v. FCC* (D.C. Cir. 2002), 01-1198, released Oct. 22, 2002.

25. FCC 96-388, *In the Matter of Implementation of the Pay Telephone Reclassification and Compensation Provisions of the Telecommunications Act of 1996, Policies and Rules Concerning Operator Service Access and Pay Telephone Compensation*, CC Docket No. 96-128, and CC Docket No. 91-35, September 20, 1996.

26. *Illinois Public Telecommunications Ass'n. v. FCC*, 117 [F.3d] 555, clarified, 123 F.3d 693 (D.C. Cir. 1997).

27. *MCI Telecommunications Corp. v. FCC*, 143 F.3d 606 (D.C. Cir. 1998), [No. 97-1675, May 15, 1998]; *American Public Communications Council v. FCC*, 215 F.3d 51 (D.C. Cir. 2000); *Sprint Corp. v. FCC* (D.C. Cir. 2002) (case 01-1266).

28. Cable Television Consumer Protection and Competition Act of 1992, Pub. L. No. 102-387.

29. FCC 93-456, *Implementation of Sections 11 and 13 of the Cable Television*

Consumer Protection and Competition Act of 1992, October 22, 1993, 8 F.C.C.R. 8565, 8609, p. 109.

30. *Daniels Cablevision, Inc. v. United States*, 835 F. Supp. 1 (D.D.C. 1993).

31. FCC 99-288, *Implementation of the Cable Television Consumer Protection and Competition Act of 1992, Implementation of Cable Act Reform Provisions of the Telecommunications Act of 1996, Review of the Commission's Cable Attribution Rules, Report and Order, CS Docket No. 98-82 and CS Docket No. 96-85*, October 8, 1999.

32. *Time Warner Entertainment Co., L.P. v. FCC*, 93 F.3d 957, 979 - 980 (D.C. Cir. 1996); *Time Warner Entertainment Co., L.P. v. FCC*, 211 F.3d 1313 (D.C. Cir. 2000); and *Time Warner Entertainment Co., L.P. v. FCC*, 240 F.3d 1126 (D.C. Cir. 2001).

33. *Fox Television Stations, Inc. v. FCC*, 280 F.3d 1027 (D.C. Cir. 2002).

34. FCC 99-208, *In the Matter of Broadcast Television National Ownership Rules, Review of the Commission's Regulations Governing Television Broadcasting Television Satellite Stations Review of Policy and Rules, Report and Order, MM Docket No. 96-222, MM Docket No. 91-221, and MM Docket No. 87-8*. August 6, 1999.

35. *Gulf Power Co. v. FCC*, 208 F.3d 1263 (11th Cir. 2000) [No. 98-6222, April 11, 2000].

36. *Southern Company v. FCC*, 293 F.3d 1338 (11 Cir. 2002), and *National Cable & Telecommunications Association, Inc. v. Gulf Power Co.*, 534 U.S. 327, 151 L.Ed.2d 794, 122 S. Ct. 782 (2002).

37. These include sections 206–9, section 312, and even sections 252 and 253.

38. Section 271.

39. See FCC 99-404, *In the Matter of Application by Verizon Under Section 271 of the Telecommunications Act of 1996 To Provide In-Region, InterLATA Services in New York*, [15 FCC Rcd 3953] December 21, 1999, concurring statement of Commissioner Harold W. Furchtgott-Roth.; FCC 00-238, *In the Matter of Application by SBC Communications Inc., Southwestern Bell Telephone Company, and Southwestern Bell Communications Services, Inc. d/b/a Southwestern Bell Long Distance Pursuant to Section 271 of the Telecommunications Act of 1996 To Provide In-Region, InterLATA Services in Texas*, 15 FCC Rcd 18354, June 30, 2000; see also FCC 01-29, *In the Matter of Application by SBC Communications Inc., Southwestern Bell Telephone Company, and Southwestern Bell Communications Services, Inc. d/b/a Southwestern Bell Long Distance Pursuant to Section 271 of the Telecommunications Act of 1996 To Provide In-Region, InterLATA Services in Kansas and Oklahoma, CC Docket 00-217*, concurring statement of Commissioner Harold W. Furchtgott-Roth, January 22, 2001.

40. 47 U.S.C. 5.

41. The transfers are usually under 47 U.S.C. 214 or 310.

42. In recent years, these mergers have included Bell Atlantic–NYNEX, Bell Atlantic–GTE, MCI-WorldCom, AT&T-TCI, AT&T-MediaOne, CBS-Viacom, SBC–Pacific Telesis, SBC–Southwest New England, SBC-Ameritech, Qwest–U.S. West, Vodaphone-Airtouch, Deutsche Telekom–Voice Stream, the creation of Cingular, and AOL–Time Warner.

Chapter 9: An Appearance of Discriminatory Treatment by the FCC

1. See, e.g., 47 U.S.C., sections 271 and 272.

2. See, e.g., FCC 00-238, *In the Matter of Application by SBC Communications, Inc., Southwestern Bell Telephone Company, and Southwestern Bell Communications Services, Inc., d/b/a Southwestern Bell Long Distance Pursuant to Section 271 of the Telecommunications Act of 1996 To Provide In-Region, InterLATA Services in Texas, CC Docket No. 00-65*, Concurring Statement of Commissioner Harold W. Furchtgott-Roth. June 30, 2000.

3. For a summary history, see FCC 00-396, *Second Report and Order in CC Docket No. 99-139 and Order in CC Docket No. 99-117*; and *AAD File No. 98-26*; adopted November 1, 2000.

4. See Christopher Stern, "FCC Chairman Reexamines Deregulation Agency to Keep Disclosure Requirements," *Washington Post*, August 17, 2002.

5. See H. Furchtgott-Roth, letter to the editor, *Washington Post*, September 7, 2002.

6. See FCC 99-380, *Memorandum Opinion, and Order*, adopted December 1, 1999. See also *QWEST Communications, Inc. v. FCC*, 229 F.3d 1172 (D.C. Cir. 2000).

7. H. Furchtgott-Roth, "The FCC's Investigation of 'Subliminal Techniques:' From the Sublime to the Absurd," FCC press statement, September 19, 2000.

8. 47 U.S.C. 258.

9. FCC 98-334, *In the Matter of Implementation of the Subscriber Carrier Selection Changes Provisions of the Telecommunications Act of 1996 Policies and Rules Concerning Unauthorized Changes of Consumers' Long Distance Carriers, CC Docket No. 94-129, Second Report and Order, and Further Notice of Proposed Rulemaking*, adopted December 17, 1998.

10. See, for example, FCC 98-146, *In the Matter of All American Telephone Company Apparent Liability for Forfeiture, Notice of Apparent Liability, File No. ENF-98-09, NAL/Acct. No. 816EF0008*, adopted July 6, 1998.

11. The Clayton Act is the federal antitrust law prohibiting mergers that lessen competition. The FCC is one of the federal agencies with limited enforcement power of the Clayton Act. See 15 U.S.C. 21.

12. 47 U.S.C. 214, 308, 309, and 310. The fullest explanation of the FCC's asserted authority to review mergers and impose unrelated conditions under the "public interest doctrine" is found in the Bell Atlantic–NYNEX merger. See FCC 97-286, *In Re the Applications of NYNEX Corporation (Transferor), and Bell Atlantic Corporation (Transferee), for Consent to Transfer Control of NYNEX Corporation and Its Subsidiaries, Memorandum Opinion and Order*, August 14, 1997.

13. E.g., the acquisition of Capital Cities–ABC by Disney, or the acquisition of CBS by Westinghouse.

14. Some of the early mergers after the passage of the Act included U.S. West–Continental Cablevision (handled by the Cable Bureau), and SBC–Pacific Telesis.

15. FCC 97-286, Bell Atlantic–NYNEX.

16. Ibid.

17. See FCC Merger En Banc Hearing (CC Docket No. 98-141, CC Docket 98-141, and CS Docket 98-178), (December 14, 1998) and FCC *En Banc Hearing, Applications of America Online, Inc. and Time Warner, Inc. for Transfers of Control (CS Docket No. 00-30)*, July 27, 2000.

18. The stipulated conditions mentioned in the order approving the license transfer are contained in appendices C and D of FCC 97-286. Needless to say, none of the conditions is a simple restatement of obligations under the prevailing law of the time. Instead, the conditions imposed additional company-specific obligations on the newly merged Bell Atlantic.

19. See H. Furchtgott-Roth, "Can-Opener Merger Review Law," (keynote address to the American Law Institute, American Bar Association, New York City, October 5, 2000).

20. See FCC Web site, Office of General Counsel, http://www.fcc.gov/transaction (accessed October 17, 2005).

21. See FCC, *Applications of Ameritech Corp. (Transferor) and SBC Communications, Inc. (Transferee), for Consent to Transfer Control of Corporations Holding Commission Licenses and Lines Pursuant to Sections 214 and 310(d) of the Communications Act and Parts 5, 22, 24, 25, 63, 90, 95, and 101 of the Commission's Rules, CC Docket 98-141*, statement of H. Furchtgott-Roth, concurring in part and dissenting in part, October 6, 1999. This statement uses these eleven deficiencies as headings.

22. House Committee on the Judiciary, Subcommittee on Commercial and Administrative Law, "Hearing on Novel Procedures for License Transfer Proceedings," 106th Cong., 1st sess., May 25, 1999. See, in particular, testimony of H. Furchtgott-Roth.

23. House Committee on Commerce, Subcommittee on Telecommunications, Trade, and Consumer Protection, "Hearing on the Telecommunications Merger Review Act of 2000," 106th Cong., 2d sess., Serial No. 106-95, March 14, 2000. See, in particular, testimony of H. Furchtgott-Roth.

24. For a history of the applications, see *Sinclair Broadcast Group v. FCC*, Petition for Issuance of Writ of Mandamus, September 10, 2001, Dkt. No. 01-1397 (D.C. Cir. 2001).

25. FCC 01-336, *In the Matter of Edwin L. Edwards, Sr. (Transferor) and Carolyn C. Smith (Transferee) for Consent to the Transfer of Control of Glencairn, Ltd. (Sinclair)*, Memorandum Opinion and Order and Notice of Apparent Liability, adopted November 15, 2001.

26. *Sinclair Broadcast Group v. FCC*, Petition for Issuance of Writ of Mandamus, September 10, 2001, Dkt. No. 01-1397 (D.C. Cir. 2001).

27. Ibid.

28. See FCC 99-393, *WQED Pittsburgh, Memorandum Opinion and Order*, adopted December 15, 1999.

29. Ibid.

30. See FCC 00-25, *WQED Pittsburgh, Order on Reconsideration*, adopted January 28, 2000.

31. See separate statement of H. Furchtgott-Roth, in FCC, DA 99-1200, *In re Applications of AirTouch Communications, Inc. (Transferor) and Vodafone Group, PLC. (Transferee), for Consent to Transfer of Control of Licenses and Authorizations, File Nos. 0000003690, et al., Memorandum Opinion and Order, by the Chief Wireless Telecommunications Bureau,* June 21, 1999.

32. FCC 02-284, *Re EchoStar Communications Corporation, General Motors Corporation, and Hughes Electronics Corporation (Transferors) and EchoStar Communications Corporation (Transferee),* (CS Docket 01-348), Hearing Designation Order, October 18, 2002.

33. House Committee on Commerce, Subcommittee on Telecommunications, Trade, and Consumer Protection, "Hearing on the Telecommunications Merger Review Act of 2000." See, in particular, testimony of M. Powell.

34. See, particularly, Comcast-AT&T.

35. See comment of Commissioner H. Furchtgott-Roth at FCC Merger En Banc Hearing (CC Docket No. 98-141, CC Docket 98-141, and CS Docket 98-178), December 14, 1998.

36. See FCC Web site, Office of General Counsel, www.fcc.gov/ogc.

37. BellAtlantic in New York in December 1999 was the first BOC to receive FCC approval to offer interLATA services. Qwest in Arizona in December 2003 was the last.

38. 47 U.S.C. section 271.

39. Ibid., section 271(d)(4).

40. In particular, sections 251 and 252 of the Act, as referenced in section 271.

41. FCC 99-404, *Re Application by Bell Atlantic New York for Authorization Under Section 271 of the Communications Act To Provide In-Region, InterLATA Service in the State of New York,* Memorandum Opinion and Order, December 22, 1999.

42. See *AT&T Corp. v. FCC,* F.3d 607 (D.C. Cir. 2000).

43. FCC 99-168, *In the Matter of Low-Volume Long Distance Users, Notice of Inquiry,* adopted July 8, 1999.

44. FCC 99-119, *In the Matter of Federal-State Joint Board on Universal Service, Access Charge Reform, Seventh Report & Order and Thirteenth Order on Reconsideration in CC Docket No. 96-45, Fourth Report & Order in CC Docket No. 96-262, and Further Notice of Proposed Rulemaking,* adopted May 27, 1999; FCC 99-120, *In the Matter of Federal-State Joint Board on Universal Service, Forward Looking Mechanism for High Cost Support for Non-Rural LECs, Further Notice of Proposed Rulemaking,* adopted May 27, 1999; and FCC 99-121, *In the Matter of Federal-State Joint Board on Universal Service, Twelfth Order on Reconsideration in CC Docket No. 96-45,* adopted May 27, 1999;

45. See FCC, "Access Charges Cut, Lower Long-Distance Rates Should Follow," press release, June 29, 1999; and FCC, "Press Statement of Commissioner Furchtgott-Roth Regarding Reduction in Access Charges," press release, June 30, 1999.

46. The original CALLS proposal was presented to the FCC in July 1999 and formally restated for the public in FCC 99-235, *In the Matter of Access Charge Reform, Price Cap Review for Local Exchange Carriers, Low-Volume Long-Distance Users, and Federal-State Joint Board on Universal Service*, adopted September 14, 1999.

47. See, e.g., H. Furchtgott-Roth, "FCC Votes to Raise E-Rate Tax by $1 Billion. FCC Again Violates Statutory Mandate By Increasing E-Rate Tax While Delaying Implementation of High-Cost Program," press release, May 28, 1999; and comments before the Minnesota Association for Rural Telecommunications, Minneapolis, Minnesota, October 14, 1999; "Competition and Regulation" (David T. Chase Free Enterprise Institute Lecture, Eastern Connecticut State University, Willimantic, Conn., April 26, 2000); "The *Realpolitik* of Regulation: Offensive and Defensive Strategies," (lecture, American Enterprise Institute Amgen Forum, Washington, D.C., April 28, 2000); "Competition for Regulatory Ideas," (comments, National Association of Regulatory Utility Commissioners, Los Angeles, Calif., July 25, 2000).

48. FCC 99-168, July 8, 1999.

49. See dissenting statement of H. Furchtgott-Roth in FCC 00-183, *In the Matter of the Implementation of the Local Competition Provisions of the Telecommunications Act of 1996, Supplemental Order Clarification*, adopted May 19, 2000.

50. The FCC revised the list of unbundled network elements in response to the Supreme Court decision in *AT&T Corp. v. Iowa Utilities Board*, 119 S. Ct. (1999). See FCC 99-238, *In the Matter of the Implementation of Local Competition Provisions of the Telecommunications Act of 1996, Third Report and Order and Fourth Further Notice of Proposed Rulemaking*, September 15, 1999. Many ILECs wanted to prohibit specific combinations of elements, known as EELs, even though the statutory language of section 251 specifically permits ILECs to bundle elements at their discretion. See dissenting statement of H. Furchtgott-Roth. Nonetheless, the D.C. Circuit Court of Appeals upheld the FCC decision with respect to EELs in response to a challenge by the Competitive Telecommunications Association. See *Competitive Telecommunications Ass'n. v. FCC*, 309 F.3d 8 (D.C. Cir. 2002).

51. The FCC initially denied the ILEC forbearance petition on depreciation rates. See FCC 397, *Review of Depreciation Requirements for Incumbent Local Exchange Carriers, Report and Order in CC Docket 98-137*, released December 30, 1999.

52. FCC 00-119, *In the Matter of the 1998 Biennial Regulatory Review—Review of Depreciation Requirements for Incumbent Local Exchange Companies; Ameritech Corporation Telephone Operating Companies' Continuing Property Records Audit, et al; GTE Telephone Operating Companies Release of Information Obtained During Joint Audit; Further Notice of Proposed Rulemaking*, adopted March 31, 2000.

53. Ibid.

54. FCC, DA 00-533, Public Notice, *Coalition for Affordable Local and Long Distance Services (CALLS) Modified Proposal, Pleading Cycle Established*, March 8, 2000.

55. See FCC 00-396, *Second Report and Order in CC Docket No. 99-139 and Order in CC Docket No. 99-117; and AAD File No. 98-26*; adopted November 1, 2000.

56. See concurring statement of H. Furchtgott-Roth in FCC 00-119.

57. At the time of the CALLS order, I made the following observation:

[The chairman] asserts that the Commission has simply considered "overlapping policy considerations" between these separate dockets. To think otherwise, he claims, is "to put blinders on" to avoid "seeing the entire landscape," preventing the Commission from "get[ting] where we want to be." But these metaphors apply far more aptly to the Commission itself. By shielding from public scrutiny the totality of the deal it made with a select group of parties with interests in the CALLS proposal, it is the Commission that wishes to blind the public to the "entire landscape." I certainly have no objection to the Commission's trying to reach a desirable outcome. I would simply like for us to reach our goals through a forthright process that is consistent with the law [footnotes omitted]. Ibid.

58. U.S. West, and subsequently Qwest, successfully challenged the FCC on two issues: (1) the release of data collected during the CPR audit, *Qwest Communications, Inc. v. FCC*, 229 F.3d 1172 (D.C. Cir. 2000); and (2) the selection of a cost model for universal service, *Qwest Corp. v. FCC*, 258 F.3d 1191 (10th Cir. 2001).

59. FCC 99-235, September 14, 1999.

Chapter 10: The Miracle of Compound Interests

1. Initially, the FCC limited designated entities to small businesses and woman- and minority-owned firms. Small, rural telephone companies were sometimes excluded from designated-entity status, except under the other criteria.

2. *Adarand v. Pena*, 515 U.S. 200 (1995).

3. See various FCC orders from 1994 through 1996.

4. FCC 97-417, *In the Matter of Carolina PCS I Limited Partnership Request for Waiver of Section 24.711(a)(2) of the Commission's Rules Regarding BTA Nos. B016, B072, B091, B147, B177, B178, B312, B335, and B436, Frequency Block C, Memorandum Opinion and Order*, December 24, 1997.

5. See, e.g., FCC, DA 98-547, Public Notice, *Commission Staff Requests Submission of Superior Alternatives to Proposed Agreement to Resolve Pocket Communications Bankruptcy, In Re Pocket Communications, Inc., No. 97-5-4105-ESD, and In Re DCR PCS, Inc.*, released March 23, 1998.

6. FCC, statement from FCC Chairman William E. Kennard on the appeal filed by the U.S. Department of Justice from the April 24, 1998 ruling in the GWI bankruptcy case by the U.S. Bankruptcy Court (N.D. Texas), June 8, 1998.

7. Ibid.

8. FCC, DA Number: 98-1897, Wireless Bureau, Guidance on Grace Period and Installment Payment Rules, September 18, 1998.

9. See, e.g., FCC 94-28, *In the Matter of the Implementation of Section 309(j) of the Communications Act-Competitive Bidding, Fifth Memorandum Opinion and Order,* adopted November 10, 1994:

> In the event an entrepreneurs' block licensee becomes subject to bank-ruptcy, our existing rules and precedent clarify how the Commission would dispose of a license in such a circumstance. Specifically, trans-fer to a bankruptcy trustee is viewed as an involuntary transfer or assignment to another party under Section 24.839 of the Commission's Rules. In such a case therefore, there would be a pro forma involun-tary assignment of the license to a court-appointed trustee in bank-ruptcy, or to the licensee, as a debtor-in-possession. Assuming the bankrupt estate is liquidated or the trustee finds a qualified purchaser for the licensee's system, and assuming payments to the Commission are maintained or a grace period granted, we will continue generally to defer to federal bankruptcy laws on many matters. We would, how-ever, ultimately have to approve any final transfer of the license. As stated above, we would expect that any requirements that arise by virtue of a licensee's status as an entrepreneur or as a designated entity would be satisfied with respect to such a sale. Thus, for example, the transfer would need to be to another qualified entrepreneur if it is to occur within our five-year holding period.

10. FCC 97-342, *In the Matter of Amendments of the Commission's Rules Regarding Installment Payment Financing for Personal Communications Services (PCS) Licenses, Second Report and Order and Further Notice of Proposed Rule Making,* adopted Sep-tember 25, 1997.

11. FCC, WT Docket 97-82, *In the Matter of Requests for Extension of the Com-mission's Initial Non-Delinquency Period for C and F Block Installment Payments,* Octo-ber 29, 1998.

12. FCC, WT Docket 97-82, *In the Matter of Requests for Extension of the Commission's Initial Non-Delinquency Period for C and F Block Installment Payments,* March 25, 1999.

13. *NextWave Personal Communications, Inc. v. FCC,* 254 F.3d 130 (D.C. Cir. 2001).

14. See statement of Chairman M. K. Powell, *Re: Disposition of Down Payments and Pending Applications By Certain Winning Bidders in Auction No. 35,* November 14, 2002.

15. *FCC v. NextWave Personal Communications, Inc.,* No. 01-653 (S. Ct. 2003).

Conclusion

1. See in particular efforts for the transition of digital television and the timing of spectrum auctions.

2. See *AT&T Corp. v. Iowa Utilities Board*, 119 S. Ct. (1999), 738.

3. Fifth Circuit Court, *Texas Office of Public Utility Counsel et al. v. FCC*, No. 97-60421, decision issued July 30, 1999.

4. See, e.g., C. S. Yoo, S. G. Calabresi, and L. Nee, "The Unitary Executive During the Third Half-Century, 1889–1945," http://law.vanderbilt.edu/faculty/pubs/yoo-unitaryexecduringthirdhalfcentury.pdf (accessed November 24, 2004).

5. Ibid.

6. Alexis de Tocqueville, *Democracy in America*, trans. and ed. Harvey C. Mansfield and Delba Winthrop (Chicago: University of Chicago Press, 2000), 216.

Appendix

1. FCC, DA 96-2039, *In the Matter of MFS Communications Company, Inc. and WorldCom, Inc. Application for Authority Pursuant to Section 214 of the Communications Act of 1934, as Amended, to Transfer Control of International Authorizations Eagle Uplink Corporation Application for Authority Pursuant to Section 25.118 of the Commission's Rules to Transfer Control of Earth Station Licenses, Memorandum Opinion, Order, and Authorization*, December 5, 1996.

2. FCC 97-28, *In re Applications of Pacific Telesis Group (Transferor) and SBC Communications, Inc. (Transferee), for Consent to Transfer Control of Pacific Telesis Group and Its Subsidiaries, Memorandum Opinion and Order*, January 31, 1997.

3. FCC 97-286, *In re Applications of NYNEX Corporation (Transferor) and Bell Atlantic Corporation (Transferee), for Consent to Transfer Control of NYNEX Corporation and Its Subsidiaries, Memorandum Opinion and Order*, August 14, 1997.

4. FCC, International Bureau, Public Notice, I-8307, ITC-98-271, *Transfer of Control Application for Authority to Transfer Control of LCI International Telecom Corp. (LCIT) and USLD Communications, Inc. (USLDI) from the Current Shareholder of LCI International, Inc. (LCII) to Qwest*, May 21, 1998.

5. FCC 98-169, *In re Applications of Teleport Communications Group, Inc. (Transferor) and AT&T Corp. (Transferee), for Consent to Transfer Control of Corporations Holding Point-To-Point Microwave Licenses and Authorizations to Provide International Facilities-Based and Resold Communications Services*, adopted July 21, 1998.

6. FCC 98-225, *In the Matter of the Application of WorldCom Inc. and MCI Communications Corporation for Transfer of Control of MCI Communications Corporation to WorldCom Inc., Memorandum Opinion and Order*, September 14, 1998.

7. FCC 98-276, *In the Matter of Applications for Consent to the Transfer of Control of Licenses and Section 214 Authorizations from Southern New England Telecommunications Corporation (Transferor) to SBC Communications, Inc. (Transferee)*, October 23, 1998.

8. FCC 99-279, *In re Applications of Ameritech Corp. (Transferor) and SBC Communications, Inc. (Transferee), for Consent to Transfer Control of Corporations Holding Commission Licenses and Lines Pursuant to Sections 214 and 310(d) of the Communications Act and Parts 5, 22, 24, 25, 63, 90, 95, and 101 of the Commission's Rules, Memorandum Opinion and Order*, October 6, 1999.

9. FCC 99-313, *In the Matter of AT&T Corp., British Telecommunications, plc, VLT Co. L.L.C., Violet License Co. LLC, and TNV [Bahamas] Limited Applications for Grant of Section 214 Authority, Modification of Authorizations and Assignment of Licenses in Connection with the Proposed Joint Venture Between AT&T Corp. and British Telecommunications, plc, Memorandum Opinion and Order*, October 22, 1999.

10. FCC 00-91, *In the Matter of Qwest Communications International Inc. and U.S. West, Inc. Applications for Transfer of Control of Domestic and International Sections 214 and 310 Authorizations and Application to Transfer Control of a Submarine Cable Landing License, Memorandum Opinion and Order*, March 8, 2000.

11. FCC 00-221, *In re Application of GTE Corporation (Transferor), and Bell Atlantic Corporation (Transferee) for Consent to Transfer Control of Domestic and International Sections 214 and 310 Authorizations and Application to Transfer Control of a Submarine Cable Landing License, Memorandum Opinion and Order*, June 16, 2000.

12. FCC, DA 00-2783, *In the Matter of Joint Applications of OnePoint Communications Corp. and Verizon Communications for Authority Pursuant to Section 214 of the Communications Act of 1934, as Amended, To Transfer Control of Authorizations to Provide Domestic Interstate and International Telecommunications Services as a Non-Dominant Carrier, Memorandum Opinion and Order*, December 8, 2000.

13. FCC, DA 01-130, *In the Matter of Intermedia Communications Inc., Transferor, and WorldCom, Inc., Transferee, for Consent to Transfer Control of Corporations Holding Commission Licenses and Authorizations Pursuant to Sections 214 and 310(d) of the Communications Act and Parts 21, 63, 90, 101, Memorandum Opinion and Order*, January 17, 2001.

14. FCC, DA 01-961, *In the Matter of Joint Applications of Global Crossing Ltd., and Citizens Communications Company for Authority To Transfer Control of Corporations Holding Commission Licenses and Authorizations Pursuant to Sections 214 and 310(d) of the Communications Act and Parts 20, 22, 63, 78, 90, and 101 of the Commission's Rules, Memorandum Opinion and Order*, April 16, 2001.

15. FCC, DA 01-1914, *In the Matter of Joint Applications of Telephone and Data Systems, Inc. and Chorus Communications, Ltd. for Authority to Transfer Control of Commission Licenses and Authorizations Pursuant to Sections 214 and 310(d) of the Communications Act and Parts 22, 63 and 90 of the Commission's Rules, Memorandum Opinion and Order*, August 10, 2001.

16. FCC, DA 02-2512, *In re Applications of XO Communications Inc. for Consent to Transfer Control of Licenses and Authorizations Pursuant to Sections 214 and 310(d) of the Communications Act and Petition for Declaratory Ruling Pursuant to Section*

310(b)(4) of the Communications Act, Memorandum, Opinion, Order, and Authoriza-tion, October 3, 2002.

17. FCC 99-24, *In the Matter of Applications for Consent to Transfer of Control of Licenses and Section 214 Authorizations from Tele-Communications Inc. (Transferor) to AT&T Corp. (Transferee), Memorandum Opinion and Order*, February 17, 1999.

18. FCC 00-202, *In the Matter of Applications for Consent to the Transfer of Control of Licenses and Section 214 Authorizations from MediaOne Group, Inc. (Transferor), to AT&T Corp. (Transferee), Memorandum Opinion and Order*, June 5, 2000.

19. FCC 01-12, *In the Matter of Applications for Consent to the Transfer of Control of Licenses and Section 214 Authorizations by Time Warner Inc. and America Online Inc. (Transferors), to AOL Time Warner Inc. (Transferee), Memorandum Opinion and Order*, January 11, 2001.

20. FCC 02-310, *In the Matter of Applications for Consent to the Transfer of Control of Licenses from Comcast Corporation and AT&T Corp (Transferors) to AT&T Comcast Corporation (Transferee), Memorandum Opinion and Order*, November 14, 2002

21. FCC 00-277, *In the Matter of Lockheed Martin Corporation, COMSAT Govern-ment Systems, LLC, and COMSAT Corporation Applications for Transfer of Control of COMSAT Corporation and Its Subsidiaries, Licensees of Various Satellite, Earth Station Private Land Mobile Radio and Experimental Licenses, and Holders of International Sec-tion 214 Authorizations, Order and Authorizations*, July 27, 2000.

22. DA 01-2100, *In re Application of General Electric Capital Corporation (Trans-ferors), and SES Global, S.A. (Transferees), for Consent to Transfer Control of Licenses and Authorizations Pursuant to Sections 214(a) and 310(d) of the Communications Act and Petition for Declaratory Ruling Pursuant to Section 310(b)(4) of the Communications Act, Order and Authorization*, October 1, 2001.

23. FCC 01-369, *In the Matter of Lockheed Martin Global Telecommunications, Com-sat Corporation, and Comsat General Corporation (Assignor) and Telenor Satellite Mobile Services, Inc., and Telenor Satellite, Inc. (Assignee), Applications for Assignment of Section 214 Authorizations, Private Land Mobile Radio Licenses, Experimental Licenses, and Earth Station Licenses and Petition for Declaratory Ruling Pursuant to Section 310(b)(4) of the Communications Act, Order and Authorization*, December 14, 2001.

24. DA 02-307, *In re Applications of Space Station System Licensee, Inc. (Assignor), and Iridium Constellation, LLC (Assignee), for Consent to Assignment of License Pursuant to Section 310(d) of the Communications; Memorandum Opinion, Order and Authoriza-tion*, February 8, 2002.

25. DA 02-576, *In re Application of Orbital Communications Corporation and ORB-COMM GLOBAL, L.P. (ASSIGNORS) for Consent to Assign Non-Common Carrier Earth and Space Station Authorizations, Experimental Licenses, and VSAT Network to ORB-COMM License Corp. and ORBCOMM LLC (Assignees), Order and Authorization*, March 8, 2002.

26. FCC, DA 99-1200, *In re Applications of AirTouch Communications, Inc. (Trans-feror) and Vodafone Group, PLC. (Transferee), for Consent to Transfer of Control of*

Licenses and Authorizations, File Nos. 0000003690, et al., Memorandum Opinion and Order, by the Chief *Wireless Telecommunications Bureau,* June 21, 1999.

27. FCC, DA 99-1318, *In re Applications of Comcast Cellular Holdings Co. (Transferor), and SBC Communications, Inc. (Transferee), for Consent to Transfer of Control of Licenses and Authorizations, Memorandum Opinion and Order,* July 2, 1999.

28. FCC 00-53, *In re Applications of VoiceStream Wireless Corporation or Omnipoint Corporation (Transferors), Cook Inlet/VS GSM II PCS, LLC, Cook Inlet/VS GSMIII PCS, LLC (Transferees), and Various Subsidiaries and Affiliates of Omnipoint Corporation (Assignor) and Cook Inlet/VS GSM II PCS, LLC, Cook Inlet/VS GSMIII PCS, LLC (Assignees), for Consent to Transfer of Control and Assignment of Licenses and Authorizations, Memorandum Opinion and Order,* February 14, 2000.

29. FCC, DA 00-925, *In the Matter of Arch Communications Group, Inc., and Paging Network, Inc., for Consent to Transfer Control of Paging, Narrowband PCS, and Other Licenses, Memorandum Opinion and Order,* April 25, 2000.

30. FCC, DA 00-2223, *In re Applications of SBC Communications, Inc., and Bell-South Corporation for Consent to Transfer of Control or Assignment of Licenses and Authorizations, Memorandum Opinion and Order,* September 29, 2000.

31. FCC, DA 00-2443, *In re Applications of TeleCorp PCS, Inc., Tritel, Inc., and Indus, Inc., and TeleCorp Holding Corp. II, LLC, TeleCorp PCS, LLC, ABC Wireless, LLC, PolyCell Communications, Inc., Clinton Communications, Inc., and AT&T Wireless PCS, LLC, for Consent to Transfer of Control and Assignment of Licenses and Authorizations and Royal Wireless, LLC, and Zuma PCS, LLC, for Consent to Transfer of Control Licenses and Authorizations and Southwest Wireless, LLC, Poka Lambro Ventures, Inc., Poka Lambro PCS, Inc., Poka Lambro/PVT Wireless, L.P., and Denton County Electric Cooperative, Inc., for Consent to Assignment of Licenses and Authorizations, Memorandum Opinion and Order,* October 27, 2000.

32. FCC, DA 00-2820 *In re Applications of Cook Inlet Region, Inc. (Transferor) and VoiceStream Wireless Corporation (Transferee) for Consent to Transfer of Control of Licenses and Authorizations and for Consent to Transfer an International Section 214 Authorization and Cook Inlet/VoiceStream PCS, LLC, et al., Applicants Petition for Declaratory Ruling Under Section 310(b)(4) of the Communications Act of 1934, as Amended, Order,* December 13, 2000

33. FCC, *Wireless Telecommunications Bureau Assignment of Authorization and Transfer of Control Applications Action, Report Number 793,* February 28, 2001.

34. FCC, DA 00-2352, *In re Applications of Motorola, Inc.; Motorola SMR, Inc.; and Motorola Communications and Electronics, Inc. (Assignors); and FCI 900, Inc. (Assignee), for Consent to Assignment of 900 MHz Specialized Mobile Radio Licenses, Order,* April 16, 2001.

35. FCC 01-142, *VoiceStream Wireless Corporation, Powertel, Inc. (Transferors), and Deutsche Telekom AG (Transferee), for Consent to Transfer Control of Licenses and Authorizations Pursuant to Sections 214 and 310(d) of the Communications Act and Petition for Declaratory Ruling Pursuant to Section 310 of the Communications Act and*

Powertel, Inc. (Transferor) and VoiceStream Wireless Corporation (Transferee), for Consent to Transfer Control of Licenses and Authorizations Pursuant to Sections 214 and 310(d) of the Communications Act and Eliska Wireless Ventures License Subsidiary I, LLC, Wireless Alliance, LLC, Cook Inlet/VS GSM IV PCS, LLC, and Cook Inlet/VS GSM V PCS, LLC, Petitions for Declaratory Ruling Pursuant to Section 310(b)(4) of the Communications Act and Iowa Wireless Services Holding Corporation, et al. Petition for a Declaratory Ruling Pursuant to Section 310(b)(4) of the Act, and for a Ruling that the Transfer of a Minority Ownership Interest in the Licensee Does Not Constitute a Transfer of Control under Section 310(d), Memorandum Opinion and Order, April 24, 2001.

36. FCC, DA 01-1268, *In re Application of AWI Spectrum Co., LLC (Assignor); and ACI 900, Inc. (Assignee), for Consent to Assignment of Specialized Mobile Radio Licenses, Order,* May 25, 2001.

37. FCC, DA 01-2685, *In re Applications of Pacific Wireless Technologies, Inc., and Nextel of California, Inc., for Consent to Assignment of Licenses, Memorandum Opinion and Order,* November 16, 2001.

38. FCC, DA 01-2765, *In re Applications of Chadmoore Wireless Group, Inc., and Various Subsidiaries of Nextel Communications, Inc., for Consent to Assignment of Licenses, Memorandum Opinion and Order,* November 30, 2001.

39. FCC, DA 02-331, Public Notice, *Wireless Telecommunications Bureau and International Bureau Grant Consent for the Transfer of Control or Assignment of Licenses from Telecorp PCS, Inc., to AT&T Wireless Services, Inc.,* February 12, 2002.

40. FCC, DA 02-1366, Public Notice, *Wireless Telecommunications Bureau Grants Consent for the Transfer of Licenses from CenturyTel, Inc., to ALLTEL Communications, Inc.,* June 12, 2002.

41. FCC 96-495, *In re Applications of Stockholders of Infinity Broadcasting Corporation (Transferor) and Westinghouse Electric Corporation (Transferee); for Transfer of Control, Memorandum Opinion and Order,* December 26, 1996.

42. FCC 00-155, *In the Matter of the Applications of Shareholders of CBS Corporation, (Transferor) and Viacom, Inc., (Transferee) for Transfer of Control of CBS Corporation and Certain Subsidiaries, Licensees of KCBS-TV, Los Angeles, CA., et al., Memorandum Opinion and Order,* May 3, 2000.

43. FCC 00-296, *In the Matter of the Applications of Shareholders of AMFM, Inc. (Transferor) and Clear Channel Communications, Inc. (Transferee), for Consent to the Transfer of Control, Memorandum Opinion and Order,* August 7, 2000.

44. FCC 01-209, *In the Matter of the Applications of UTV of San Francisco, Inc., KCOP Television, Inc., UTV of San Antonio, Inc., Oregon Television, Inc., UTV of Baltimore, Inc., WWOR-TV, Inc., and UTV of Orlando, Inc. and United Television, Inc. (Assignors) and Fox Television Stations, Inc. (Assignee) for Consent to the Assignment of Licenses, Memorandum Opinion and Order,* July 23, 2001.

45. FCC 01-336, *In the Matter of Edwin L. Edwards, Sr. (Transferor) and Carolyn C. Smith (Transferee) for Consent to the Transfer of Control of Glencairn, Ltd. (Sinclair),*

Memorandum Opinion and Order and Notice of Apparent Liability, adopted November 15, 2001.

46. FCC 02-113, *In the Matter of Telemundo Communications Group, Inc. (Transferor) and TN Acquisition Corp. (Transferee), for Consent to the Transfer of Control, Memorandum Opinion and Order*, April 9, 2002.

Index

About the Author

Harold Furchtgott-Roth was a commissioner of the Federal Communications Commission from 1997 through 2001. Previously, he served as chief economist for the House Committee on Commerce and was a principal staff member responsible for developing the Telecommunications Act of 1996. He founded Furchtgott-Roth Economic Enterprises, an economic consulting firm, in 2003. He writes a weekly column for the business page of the *New York Sun*. This book was written while he was a visiting fellow at the American Enterprise Institute (2001–03). Mr. Furchtgott-Roth is the author of dozens of publications and the coauthor of three books. He received a PhD in economics from Stanford University and an SB in economics from the Massachusetts Institute of Technology. He and his wife, Diana, reside in Chevy Chase, Maryland with their six children.